My Love Affair with Sicily

Also by Margie Miklas

Memoirs of a Solo Traveler - My Love Affair with Italy

My Love Affair with Sicily

by

Margie Miklas

Printed in the United States of America

First Printing, April 2014

Cover photo by Margie Miklas

Edited by Almut Metzroth

For my parents, Arthur and Phyllis Longano,
who encouraged all of their children
to choose self-reliance and their individual paths in life.

ACKNOWLEDGMENTS

As my long career in critical-care nursing comes to a close, I look forward to increased traveling and writing. Enthusiastic comments by readers of my first book, as well as my blog, solidified my resolve to make writing my second career. Thank you.

I want to express my gratitude especially to my earliest and constant sources of inspiration and support:

Heartfelt thanks to my discerning and hard-working editor, Almut Metzroth, whose meticulous skills have been invaluable.

Love to my parents, Arthur Longano and Phyllis Longano, who have been faithful readers of my blog and an endless source of encouragement to me throughout my life.

With appreciation and love to my family, here and in Sicily, for validating my enthusiasm of my Sicilian roots and of the culture and lifestyle that is Sicily.

Thank you, Alfredo Vinci, for your valued suggestions about your home town of Siracusa.

For your enthusiasm and language skills, for proofreading and correcting my Italian translations, thank you, Jack DiGiorgio.

To all those whom I have come to know through social media for your 24/7 encouragement and promotion, I express my gratitude.

Table of Contents

The Early Years

The Early Years

I like the fact that I am Sicilian. What I mean is: I am an American, but my ancestry is Italian, specifically Sicilian, on my mother's side of the family. My father's parents were Italian too, but they came from the area near Campobasso in the Molise region of mainland Italy.

I remember growing up feeling that being Sicilian was something special and personal to me long before I had ever gone there. I guess that I had heard so much about it from my maternal grandmother and other relatives on that side of the family.

Grandma Savoca was born in a small village, Cesarò, located in the Messina province of Sicily. I never even knew this fact until probably ten years ago. All I knew was that she and my grandfather had come from the island, and whatever traditions they maintained were borne out of their Sicilian roots.

My earliest memories of the Sicilian culture in America involved an annual Christmas party I went to as a child in Cleveland, Ohio. Members of the local Italian-American lodge gave this party. I was only four or five years of age, so my memories of these Christmas lodge parties are limited. I vaguely recall that quite a few people attended that seasonal event. The setting was a large hall, such as those used for wedding receptions. Santa Claus was there to distribute Christmas candy to the children, and after the dinner people danced.

My grandfather, Pietro Luigi Savoca, was one of the original founders of that Italian-American lodge, *Società di Mutuo Soccorso Libertà e Progresso, Cesarò-San Teodoro*. He, along with Ulderico Palumbo and Giuseppe Amato, founded this organization in January of 1917 for the purpose of perpetuating their cultural traditions from Sicily, as well as assisting each other, while they adapted to their new way of life in Cleveland. Membership was open to Sicilians who had immigrated from Cesarò and San Teodoro, both towns in the province of Messina. This membership was extended to their spouses and children, and all of their descendants. The lodge in Cleveland was typically known as *Società Libertà e Progresso* and existed until just a few years ago.

In Italian homes, food has always played a large role at family gatherings. Recipes for specific baked desserts, such as the chocolate *tetùzzi* cookies and the applesauce cake my Grandma baked, originated during her life in Sicily. I vividly remember also the distinct aroma of her homemade sauce, and her meatballs made with Romano cheese. She used to flavor her sauce with pork, allowing it to cook for hours on the stove. It was nothing short of wonderful. Many Italian-Americans refer to the spaghetti sauce as gravy, but my Sicilian grandma called it *sugo*. *Sugo* actually came from the Italian word *succo*, which meant juice. Today my Sicilian friends refer to it as *ragu*, but only when the sauce includes meat.

When I was a child, we drove to Grandma Savoca's house every Sunday for dinner with the extended family, even though our family lived approximately a half hour away. Adhering to this Sicilian tradition was expected of us. I probably didn't appreciate that family time as much when I was a young girl as I do now. In fact, many Sundays I became carsick in my seat in the back with the warm sun streaming in through the window, and feeling the warmth on my face through the side window. The elevator music of Bob Smiley played on the radio while my mom and dad talked to each other in the front seat. My twin brothers who were two years younger than I, sat also in the back of the car. As a child I hated that music as well as those car rides.

By the time I was thirteen, going on fourteen, our family moved thirty miles away from Cleveland to the much smaller town of Elyria. I wasn't so happy about moving, but I was glad I didn't have to endure those car rides every Sunday anymore. With the addition of two baby brothers our family of five had grown to seven during the past couple of years. Perhaps my parents were glad to have a little separation from family obligations.

Even after moving away from Cleveland, my own family maintained traditions that were rooted in Sicilian culture, and they always involved food. My Mom baked homemade bread at least every week, and I still recall the tantalizing smell as she removed the loaves from the hot oven. The crust was crisp, embedded with a warm buttery flavor. The bread never turned stale, even without preservatives, because it was gone by the next day. Our large family saw to that without any problems.

I recently asked my mother who is now eighty-eight years old and still very active, what she remembers about growing up Sicilian. I thought it interesting that one of the things she thinks back about the most is the freshly baked bread her own mother made. "Nothing will ever compare to the smells of the homemade bread that Grandma Savoca baked every day," my mother reminisces. "We would eat that warm bread with olive oil and pepper—mmm, mmm, good. But that bread was also a treat to eat with chunk chocolate, bought by my parents weekly at the downtown market." Now that, I believe, would be a real treat!

Memories like these awakened early my desire to trace my roots in what my grandparents called the old country. When my brother Rick announced that he and his wife, Monica, intended to visit Italy again, he asked me whether I would like to join them. I signed on immediately.

2007

From Sicily Plans to Reality:

Arrival in Taormina

The year is 2007, when my brother Rick, my sister-in-law Monica, and I plan to go to Italy in the fall. My first trip to Italy! I am thrilled to be going with them, because they are experienced travelers and know which places to visit in Italy. The reason that I pursue this interest now is because I want to seize the opportunity to travel with companions. My lack of speaking or understanding the Italian language no longer keeps me away. I am determined, though, to learn some Italian before my future trip to this country, which so fascinates me due to my heritage.

One of the places Rick, Monica, and I plan to visit is Sicily, which is a first for the three of us. There, our immediate destination is Taormina, where Angela Savoca lives. She is a Sicilian friend of mine. We maintain our earlier established online communication through Italian genealogy boards and continue to correspond by e-mail.

Angela's last name is the same as the maiden name of my mother. Her family comes from the small village of Cesarò, the birthplace of my maternal grandparents. Angela and I believe we are related but as of today still do not have documentation to prove any relationship. We no longer care, since we are now friends and consider ourselves to be family. I am eager to meet Angela in person when I go to Italy.

Taormina, a resort town on the Ionian Sea, is situated in the region of Messina on the eastern coast. According to Angela's recent letter, she is able to arrange for us three visitors to stay at the luxury hotel where she currently works and where she can obtain an incredible discount. Not only is this hotel located in the beautiful seaside resort of Taormina, but it is also designated as a five-star hotel, definitely not one we can normally afford, even with a discount. I wonder how Angela is able to obtain rooms at such a reduced rate, but she insists that she can do this, so we now have rooms booked for four nights at *ATA Capotaormina Hotel.*

I am now on an Air One non-stop flight from Naples to Sicily with Rick and Monica. After a wonderful ten days in Rome and the Amalfi Coast we arrive at the Catania airport and pick up our rental car. As the designated driver, Rick gets into the driver's seat of the Fiat Bravo and quickly gets us onto the *autostrada,* or Italian freeway, heading in the direction of Taormina. As a former Porsche race car driver, he is a natural on Sicily's streets and finds his way without a GPS to the ATA Capotaormina Hotel on *Via Nazionale.* The hotel sits on a point overlooking the Ionian Sea. By the time we arrive at 6:30PM, it is already dusk on this October evening. The hotel lobby is spacious, the largest of any of our accommodations since arriving in Italy. I have a phone number for Angela, so I call her from a courtesy phone in the hotel lobby to announce our presence. "Wait for me. I will be there soon. Get settled into your rooms." I am grateful that Angela speaks some English, since I know very little Italian.

The efficient male hotel receptionist, smartly dressed in a dark suit, directs us to our quarters. Inside our luxurious rooms we almost cannot believe what we see. Neither the apartment in Rome nor the typical Italian-sized hotel rooms in Sorrento compare to the rooms at Capotaormina. Angela's arrangements for us to stay in the resort's best rooms exceed my expectations. Even by American standards, these rooms are huge, similar to the size of a suite. Besides an entranceway, my room includes a large dressing room with enormous closets and an immense bathroom. There is also a refrigerator with a minibar. A king-size bed dominates the main bedroom; two comfortable fabric tub-design chairs, a dresser, a desk with another chair, and a table with a fresh fruit arrangement are conveniently placed. On the dresser is a plasma screen TV, not a typical amenity in Italian hotels. Even though I am staying in a room by myself, and Rick and Monica have a separate double room, each room is the same size. We all are awestruck.

Upon further exploration I see that each room includes a balcony furnished with a table and chairs. The tabletop is made of hand painted ceramic with yellow, blue, and green designs of lemons, absolutely gorgeous. The view from here is breathtaking as I am overlooking the water. To the right is the shoreline of the neighboring town of Giardini-Naxos, sparkling with lights in the twilight. Straight ahead, snow-covered Mt. Etna is towering over the surrounding countryside. The scene is truly awesome!

Half an hour after we arrive and have a chance to freshen up and settle in, Angela calls to let us know that she is in the hotel lobby. When we all meet near the reception area, we see that she is not alone but is accompanied by her best friend, Angelica. These two beautiful girls look as if they could be sisters. Both of them have black hair, although Angelica's is jet black and particularly striking; both girls are petite and dressed as if they were going out on the town. They look very chic, especially in comparison to the three of us.

Angela knows only a little English and Angelica speaks only Italian, but their radiant faces communicate their emotions, and we offer to take them to dinner. Angela indicates that she will drive her car, and we can follow in our rental car. She drives to her home, which is in the lower part of Taormina, where Teresa, Angela's older sister, waits inside for us. They share the second-floor apartment of a grey-colored stone building. I am surprised to find their home so spacious. Most hotel rooms in Italy are small so I assume that most homes are also small, but that is not always the reality.

Their *casa* has three bedrooms, a large kitchen, a living room, which also serves as the dining room, a spacious bathroom, a hall, and two balconies. Of course the house is extremely clean and tastefully decorated with warm colors. After we spend a little time with each other, we take some photos. Amid smiles and laughter, we share Italian and English versions of life. We all enjoy this first-time encounter with these three Sicilian women, and the language barrier is not a problem.

Afterward we drive the short distance along the beach to Giardini-Naxos, the town nearby. Here we are going to a restaurant, which Angela recommends: *La Bussola*, meaning compass. That seems an appropriate name for an establishment on the water. Our three companions for tonight appear to be frequent guests at La Bussola, because the owner and his waiter immediately usher us inside with big smiles and hugs for our Sicilian friends. Obviously they recognize each other and everyone, except the three *Americanos*, starts to laugh and talk very fast in Sicilian dialect. I can see that Angelica, who is quite vivacious and especially attractive, draws the most attention from these Sicilian gentlemen. The evening promises to be interesting.

The menu looks enticing with quite a few variations of pastas and pizzas, some of which I discover for the first time. Since Sicily is an island, most restaurants situated along the coastal towns serve an abundance of seafood. It is no surprise then that the pizzas and pasta dishes feature seafood choices. How about some pasta with sea urchin?

Or pizza with octopus? Of course pizza with anchovies is a big hit here.

Not being particularly fond of seafood, I opt for the *cotoletta veal alla milanese*, or breaded veal cutlet. The specially prepared veal is not an easy menu item to find in Italy; it may be a Sicilian specialty. When the food arrives, mine is *perfetto*, just perfect. My veal looks almost exactly like I remember from my grandmother's kitchen; it tastes like hers too. I share some with Rick, since veal is one of his favorite Italian dishes, and he shares some of his spaghetti with me. Both foods are fantastic. Each of us orders a different entrée, and our Sicilian friends offer to share their meals with Rick, Monica, and me, for a taste. I try some calamari for the first time and love it. I try also some of the margherita pizza, which is savory. With a lot of encouragement from Angela, Angelica, and Teresa, I even try the pizza with *acciughe* but find the anchovies far too salty for my taste.

One of the best meals and also one of the least expensive, the dinner at La Bussola is a favorite for me. Incredibly the bill is only eighty-four euros for six of us, including beer for Teresa and Angelica. The pasta dishes are the least expensive items on the menu, costing only five euros each. We linger at the restaurant until eleven, laughing and sharing stories, and the waiters do not seem to mind at all. Even though I am unable to understand a lot of the conversation, I am fascinated as I observe these three girlfriends catch up on each other's life with great animation. "*Ciao, Teresa. Ciao, Angelica,*" says Monica as she and Rick wave goodbye.

As I hug Angela and say goodbye to her, she hands me her umbrella. "*Ecco, prendi il mio ombrello. Ne avrete di bisogno perché piove.*" Here, take my umbrella. You will need it because it is raining.

"*Grazie*, Angela. *Ciao, ciao,*" I say.

She drives slowly ahead of us to make it easy for us to find our way back to Capotaormina Hotel. Angela is sweet, and I still am impressed with her ability to orchestrate such extravagant accommodations for us.

She also arranges for some assistance from a friend who works at the *municipio,* or town council, in Cesarò to help us when we go there later this week. I am very moved by these favors, and I feel as though I am with my family here. Everyone I meet in Sicily seems happy and very friendly. Back at our hotel we park the car and call it a night. It feels wonderful to sleep in such luxurious surroundings. I already am in love with Sicily.

Unfortunately all of us awaken the following morning feeling sick with colds and nasal congestion. The minor inconvenience does not deter us, though, from enjoying the huge breakfast spread in the formal dining room at our hotel. At 9:00AM Rick and Monica meet me in the *Naxos Restaurant*, which looks like a setting for a wedding reception. The waiters are dressed in white dinner jackets and ties. In addition to the usual juices, milk, water with fizz or without, there are various coffee combinations and even champagne. I enjoy a cappuccino, some tea, orange juice, a roll, and yogurt. It is too much really, but the liquids feel good on my throat. Although the restaurant is very large, many tables are empty, since this is the off-season.

After *colazione*, or breakfast, we explore the grounds of our hotel near the spectacular cliff-edge pool that overlooks the sea. Luscious tropical plants are in bloom all around us. A large cactus plant sprouts beautiful pink flowers. We continue to wander around the property and work our way down to the lower level. From here we discover what looks like a cave, complete with water dripping down from the ceiling and the walls. After walking through the long damp passageway with its musty odors, we find the hotel's private beach at the end. The wind is blowing and the temperature feels a little cool; yet it also feels great to be here.

At eleven o'clock we are to meet Angela, so Rick, Monica, and I head upstairs to the lobby, and find Angela in her business attire of a navy blue suit with a perfectly positioned scarf in hues of gold and navy; she looks very professional.

We politely decline her dinner invitation for this evening, begging off due to our nasal congestion, and she nods that she understands, *"Capisco."* Angela then introduces us to her manager, Tea, who approaches us from behind the reception desk. Tea is most gracious, and we now have a chance to thank her for the wonderful accommodations. We present her with a small gift, and she thanks us, *"Grazie."* She then explains in Italian that she allows Angela to take the day off tomorrow, so that she can accompany us to Cesarò. Angela smiles and is visibly pleased to receive this favor from her supervisor. What great news for us, especially since we are not familiar with the roads, and Angela can help communicate in the small village where none of the residents speaks or understands English. I hope to go to the records office to obtain some information on my relatives.

Angela offers to give us a tour outside on the terrace, which we have yet to see. "*Si, grazie, Angela,*" I say. Rick and Monica nod in agreement and we follow Angela outside. From this vantage point the view is of the Ionian Sea below, and the neighboring bay where cruise ships are docked. The scene resembles a postcard. The wind continues to blow, but the fresh air feels good. We have a clear view of the enormous Mt. Etna in the distance with snow on its peak. This 11,000-foot volcano is not only the largest in all of Europe but also the most active. Then, Angela points out a small picturesque island nearby and tells us its name, *Isola Bella,* or beautiful island.

Today is a work day for Angela so Rick, Monica, and I plan to explore the city of Taormina on our own. On Angela's recommendation, we board a complimentary shuttle bus provided by the hotel to take us to the tourist area of Taormina. Since Capotaormina is situated out on a cape, and the main part of the town is above us, we need transportation. Taormina's streets are narrow and the parking is a problem, so the suggestion to take the shuttle rather than our rental car turns out to be a good one. I am surprised that the bus is a Mercedes, not something commonly seen in America, although in Italy, Mercedes is a popular choice for buses as well as cars.

By the time we arrive at *Corso Umberto*, the main street in Taormina, the weather changes to rain, not the best condition for a walking tour of the city, especially for tourists with colds. But we are here now and bear it. I feel damp and cold. To avoid some of the rain, we duck in and out of several shops, including a small supermarket. Eventually we stop for lunch in a small place, *Ristorante il Ciclope*. All three of us order *pasta pomodoro*, pasta with tomato sauce, which is so tasty. None of us are foodies and we are quite content to eat pasta pomodoro every day because it tastes particularly good in Italy.

After lunch we continue along Corso Umberto and take pleasure in our surroundings that could provide the setting for a Hollywood film. Taormina seems magical with its plentiful boutiques and small shops. Such a beautiful city; I find it easy to understand why this place is known throughout the world as a resort town. Many past and present movie stars and celebrities make Taormina a frequent vacation stop; some of these include Woody Allen, Elizabeth Taylor, and more recently, Scarlett Johansson, and Russell Crowe.

After a while I suggest to stop in the Mocambo Tea Room, better known as Mocambo Bar, to get out of the rain. "The guide book states that this café has been in Taormina since 1952, making a name for itself during the *La Dolce Vita* years," I say. "Authors Tennessee Williams and Truman Capote were frequent visitors here."

Of course the cappuccino is perfect and the cookies are scrumptious.

At last the rain stops, and we head toward one of the most well-known landmarks in this city, the ancient Greek Theatre. By the time we reach the entrance, we realize that there is not enough time to take a tour and make it back for the 4:30PM shuttle bus to our hotel. Disappointed, Rick says, "We'll just have to come back here another time and visit this seventh-century BC amphitheatre."

"Maybe more than once," I say, "and specifically, to Taormina."

Making a stop at a *farmacia*, pharmacy, we buy some cough drops and Vicks to get us through the next few days. Usually Italian pharmacists have doctorates and speak English; they can suggest the medications needed. I personally am thrilled to find Vicks here because I think it is a wonder drug.

When we browse a town, our usual agenda includes a search for an internet café to catch the score of the Major League playoff games. Today, however, I scan the sport news in *USA Today*. "Oh no!" I say. "Last time we checked scores our Cleveland Indians were a game away from going to the World Series, but now there is no more need to check the scores." *USA Today* reports that Boston beat Cleveland. Rick, in particular, is bummed about it, since he is an avid Cleveland Indians baseball fan; he still treasures the baseball he caught at Cleveland Municipal Stadium when he was nine years old.

Feeling defeated and tired, the three of us head toward the shuttle stop and ride back to the hotel.

"We need to rest for a few hours," the nurse in me prescribes, "and then go out for dinner."

"Right, a break is just what we need," Monica says.

Refreshed, my brother, his wife, and I meet in the hotel lobby at seven o'clock. From the parking area, Rick drives to Giardini-Naxos and to what quickly becomes our favorite restaurant, La Bussola. We are surprised, however, to find it closed, so we opt for the pizzeria next door.

Monica and I share a margherita pizza; Rick orders pasta. Our meals are every bit as good as our food of the previous evening. The entire bill is only twenty euros, including bottled water, *aqua naturale*, meaning without gas or fizz. The prices in Sicily are unbelievably low, much less expensive than on the mainland.

On the way home we buy more cough medicine at another farmacia and then go back to the hotel where we all anticipate a good night's sleep.

When I enter my room, I am pleasantly surprised to find the bed turned back, and two pieces of Italian *Torrone,* or nougat candy with a note that reads, "*Buonanotte,*" Good Night. I am familiar with this sweet, toasted-almond candy, especially at Christmas time with Grandma Savoca. Because of my memories, this gesture by the hotel staff touches my heart.

Sicily feels like such a special place to me; I love it here more and more each day. Because of our hotel's proximity to the water, I hear the strong sounds of the wind from inside my room. Reminiscent of how noisy the wind can be during a hurricane, I wonder whether I can sleep. Apparently my concerns are unwarranted, since I never awaken until morning.

Well rested, I still feel sick, although my sore throat and congestion is better because of my using Vicks VapoRub and the other meds. Since I am up early, I walk downstairs to the fitness center and ride the exercise bike for thirty minutes, which feels good. I try to phone home, but no one answers, so I leave a message for my husband, Steve. At breakfast, I meet Rick and Monica, who report that they feel the same way, a little better but not a hundred percent. The dry air here may actually contribute to our sore throats.

Good news: the sun is shining. We carry out our plan and drive to the small village of *Savoca,* one of the filming locations for the movie, *The Godfather*. Rick resumes his familiar seat as the driver and off we go in our little Fiat. The drive to Savoca is an experience. The roads winding up to the hilltop town are treacherous. Poor Monica is now carsick and nauseated to the point where she decides to stay in the car once we arrive. "I am nauseous and just want to stay in the car," she says. "You two wander around without me." Rick and I feel bad for her but reassure her that we will return soon as we leave her behind inside the car.

We wander around the tiny town, and it does not take us long to find the small *Bar Vitelli,* made famous by the Francis Ford Coppolla movie, *The Godfather*. An interesting bit of trivia relates to the choice of Savoca to appear as the town of *Corleone* for the film. The real Sicilian town of Corleone, already too developed and commercialized in the early 70s, forces the use of Savoca in its place as a filming location. Bar Vitelli appears the same today as in the movie. The beaded curtains across the entry, as well as the tables and chairs on the terrace, look exactly as they do in the movie.

My brother and I walk around, take photos, and enjoy the stillness of this small village. The panorama views from this elevation are extraordinary; we can see all the way down to the sea below.

Aware that Monica is waiting for us, we return to the car without lingering too long in the town. We leave Savoca and drive down the hill in search of another nearby Sicilian village, also used in the filming of *The Godfather*.

Forza d'Agro is situated up a steep hill, and requires Rick to drive on the same type of winding roads. Unfortunately Monica cannot get a break. She has had it with the swerving road by this time, yet she is a good sport. Along the way, we must stop the car in the road, as a herd of sheep leisurely crosses the street. We are amused by this, and cannot get our cameras out fast enough. A serendipitous moment—priceless. Where in America would we see this? Possibly in Colorado but certainly not in Florida.

When we reach the top of the mountain and park the car, Monica again stays inside. Rick and I discover the church used in the movie as the setting for the wedding scene of Michael Corleone and Apollonia. The Church of Sant'Agostino is used in two of *The Godfather* films. Once more the views of the surrounding hills are fantastic from this lofty perspective.

We do not wander too far in Forza d'Agro. Rick drives us back down the hill and turns onto the road that runs along the sea. On the ride back to Taormina, Monica is able to enjoy the scenery, now that the elevation is at sea level and that the road is straight.

The three of us are awed by unusual sights we see along the way, and there are plenty examples today. One of my favorites is a truck in motion, with its rear door open. I see a side of beef, which hangs from hooks inside the vehicle. At another spot we see a parked truck with fish piled in boxes in the back; a man is selling the *pesce* to the local Sicilians. Other favorite sights are the fruit-and-vegetable trucks from which anyone can buy fresh produce out of the trucks' back doors: Freshness at its best, and the vendors save on overhead.

Hungry for lunch, we find an outdoor eatery called *Ciao Ciao Spaghetteria,* located directly alongside the water's edge. To enjoy lunch on the waterfront in Sicily is special. *Bellissima!* Very beautiful! The sea is such a deep shade of turquoise blue, and with the sun shining brightly on the water, the scene is magnificent. So is the pasta pomodoro.

After we arrive back at the hotel, we sit out on our respective terraces and appreciate the warmth of the sun while sipping Coca Cola Light, Italy's version of Diet Coke. Sitting here and enjoying the scenery is so relaxing and a pleasant change of pace from yesterday's busy day in Taormina in the rain. I am relishing this day and the time to thoroughly soak in the ambience without feeling rushed.

After a little afternoon *riposo,* or rest, we head out once again to La Bussola. When we arrive, the owner recognizes us immediately and seats us inside where we order spaghetti. I would like to order a side dish of the calamari, never having had it in my life, except a small taste two nights ago here. The calamari, however, is only available as a main entrée, or *secondi piatti,* the second course. I try my best to explain that I would like the calamari, but only as an appetizer or side dish. My Italian skills are minimal, so I am unable to properly explain what I would prefer.

The waiter brings our salads and spaghetti but never comes with the calamari, so I assume that he forgot about it. I figure that calamari as a side order must not be an option, and by the time I finish the salad and spaghetti, I am already full anyway. Just as we are ready to leave, the waiter surprisingly shows up with a huge plate of fried calamari! Not only am I completely surprised, but the look on my face apparently confuses our waiter, because he thinks I want an order as the *secondi piatti*, and he is right. I am the one who creates the problem.

I feel like I must try some of the calamari now that he brings it, but I really cannot eat much more. I find out, though, that I do enjoy it tremendously and am glad that I can taste it here in Sicily near the sea, where all the seafood served is fresh. After dinner the waiter brings us a complimentary drink, which I think is lemon granita, and it tastes delicious! I later learn that this is actually *sorbetto*, which frequently is served between courses or after dinner to cleanse the palate; a nice touch.

"That was a good dinner," Rick says. "We might have

to come back to La Bussola."

"Good idea," I say.

At the hotel I receive a note from Angela with directions for the morning. We are to meet her at her house at nine o'clock to go to Cesarò.

Exploring Cesarò

I feel excitement this morning. Rick and I hope to trace our roots. As instructed, by nine o'clock we pick up Angela at her house. Thanks to her directions, we find the address on *via Francavilla* easily. The four of us drive to Cesarò, the birthplace of my maternal grandparents, Pietro Savoca and Angelina Ragonese Savoca. Angela's mother and father live in this town too, and Angela promises to introduce us to them. I look forward to that encounter.

Cesarò is only twenty-nine kilometers away from Taormina, but because it is in the mountains, the drive there seems to take forever. In reality, the trip is only an hour and fifteen minutes. As we drive through more winding roads up to an elevation of 5000 feet, I realize how high the town of Cesarò is situated. It is a dizzying drive, and the closer we come to our destination, the colder the air becomes. But the views of the surrounding green countryside and the sheep along the road make the ride worthwhile, even for Monica, who particularly enjoys seeing the sheep.

To reach Cesarò, we must drive through *Randazzo*, and once we approach this town, built on the northern slope of Mt. Etna, I am amazed to see how much black lava rock is around. The volcanic stone here is the result of an eruption back in the early 1990s, according to our personal tour guide, Angela. Although her English is limited and our Italian is also limited, somehow we are able to understand each other in the car.

As we arrive in Cesarò my excitement grows, knowing that this is where my ancestors were born. The town is said to have a population of nearly 2,500, although it appears smaller to me. The question is, however, how many people live in the houses I see.

The first place on our agenda is the municipio, since I hope to locate some birth records there. Angela explains that we need to check in here first since it will be closed after 1:00PM, like most everything else at midday in Italy.

To our disappointment we learn that Angela's friend is not working at the municipio this particular day. Thank goodness, Angela is with us because the gentleman working here only speaks Italian, or perhaps *dialetto*

Siciliano, Sicilian dialect. Since this is my first trip to Italy I know *molto poco,* or very little, Italian. The elderly Italian gentleman does not seem that interested in doing any additional work by looking things up in the old-fashioned paper record books. There is no evidence of any digital documentation here, and Angela verifies this fact when she explains to us that none of the documents here are computerized. This is, after all, a small place in the mountains of Sicily. I feel as though I am stepping back in time when I see how much more work is involved to obtain records. The gentleman has to turn the pages of each book and scroll down handwritten lists to find the information. "So if you do not know the birth year of the person you inquire about," Rick says, "you may as well be looking for a needle in a haystack."

While here, I discover that the original certificates are not kept in this office, only the names written in a ledger with the other appropriate information. I am able to learn a lot though, including the fact that my grandmother's name is actually Angela, not Angelina. We also now have the address of my grandfather's house, since his birth record includes this relevant information. In the days of the late nineteenth century, with no hospitals close by, I am not surprised that the family home is also the place of birth.

Once we complete our mission at the municipio, Angela promptly escorts us to *via Monte Pieta 41,* the address that is the birthplace of my grandfather. We walk along the winding ancient streets, which are the size of alleys. I cannot believe this good fortune: to be actually standing here with my brother and sister-in-law by my grandfather's home on this narrow, inclined, cobblestoned street. The house looks so old and has a façade made of different types of stone. There are several homes all connected to each other with this same grey stone, and each house is identified as separate only by the doors and address numbers. I notice that Grandpa's earlier abode has a very small window and a rather short doorway. The door is made of planks of wood, which are weathered; a small window with a heavy wire screen is set in the door. Attached to the stone wall is a clothesline with one or two green clothespins on it. I imagine that laundry would hang against the front of the house. No place that I am familiar with in America looks like this.

My heart flutters a bit as I contemplate that Pietro Savoca, my grandfather, was born here more than a hundred years ago. Both my brother and I are emotionally overwhelmed just to be here, and Monica takes a picture of us standing in front of the house.

Not very long after we arrive at this address, a woman appears outside from the house next door, curious as to who and why we are here. Again I feel grateful to have Angela here to help communicate. Once this woman hears our story she pleasantly informs us that her cousin currently lives in my grandfather's former home. She also tells us that if she had a key, or if her cousin were home, we would be able to go inside. I can hardly contain myself as this is more than I could have ever imagined. We thank her and then walk down Grandpa's cobblestoned street of a hundred years ago.

Angela then drives us to one of the highest points in Cesarò, an old castle. This amazing vantage point allows us to view the entire city as well as Mt. Etna. The snow-capped peaks of this volcano at 10,500 feet present an awesome scene.

Back in town we stroll through some neighborhoods and encounter different local Sicilians, who walk about outside their homes and smile, appearing friendly towards us. The streets are so narrow here that I notice the laundry is hung from one house to another across the street, unlike at Grandpa's house. People must have schedules for their turns at the clotheslines.

There is only room for one small car to navigate these tiny streets, which date back to times when only horses or donkeys traversed them.

As we approach a square, Angela points to the church. "*Guardate*," she says, "*la chiesa dove sarebbero stati battezzati i vostri nonni.*" Look," Angela says, "in that church, *Ave Maria Assunta Chiesa*, your grandparents would have been baptized. But it is not open today."

I sense a real emotional connection here and truly feel at home. I cannot describe this wonderful feeling except to say that I am in love with Sicily and its people.

Cesarò has very few shops. Suddenly we see something in the *piazza*, or square, that makes us laugh. A truck is sitting there overloaded with all types of household goods, washbasins, brooms, buckets, as well as children's toys. The driver is adjusting the load while he waits for prospective customers. We assume that he must travel from village to village and sell his merchandise out of his truck, just like the produce vendor. Monica and I can't stop looking at the scene, one which we will never forget as long as we live.

After a while, Angela leads the way to *Bar Ragonese*, in the center of the town on *Corso Regina Margherita*. We know of this place through stories from our relatives about their trip years ago. *Ragonese* is the maiden name of my grandmother. We are eager to visit and also curious as to whether there is any relation to our family. As we enter the bar, a friendly young woman behind the counter engages in conversation with Angela in Italian. She tells Angela that she does not know if we are related but suggests that we talk with her mother-in-law who lives upstairs. She then guides us to meet the owner of this establishment.

When we reach the top of the steps, the woman from the bar speaks with the owner whom I assume to be *Signora Ragonese*. With a welcoming arm gesture, she invites the four of us inside her home. We sit down at her kitchen table and she talks to us with Angela interpreting. I don't know if they are speaking Italian or the Sicilian dialect because I can't understand either. Not much time passes before the signora asks us if we would like some lunch and we politely decline. We cannot go anywhere in Sicily without an offer of food or at least something to drink. After some time in her home, we thank her for her hospitality, and the disappointing information that we are not related to this family.

"Grazie, Signora Ragonese. Arrivederci."

I am continuously surprised that these friendly Sicilians invite us into their homes without even knowing us. After I think about it for a moment, this experience takes me back to my childhood as I recall our family offering our hospitality to others. This thoughtfulness and kindness must originate from my Sicilian heritage. I remember one Thanksgiving dinner at our house as a young teenager in northeast Ohio. My memories are quite clear about the huge blizzard preventing most of our extended family from making the trip. My parents' instructions to invite all the neighbors in for dinner still resonate in my mind today. My mother tells that story with great pride, which I appreciate. Sicilians are generous and always invite others in for food.

Once we are back on the first floor of Bar Ragonese, Giuseppe Ragonese introduces himself as the son of Signora Ragonese, and he, too, is extremely friendly. He appears to be the one who runs Bar Ragonese, and he mentions that he does not know anyone from our family. Before we leave the bar, Monica takes some tissue paper she finds there with the words Bar Ragonese imprinted on it. She tells me later that she thinks my parents might enjoy that souvenir.

Since we decline Angela's generous offer to have a meal at her home, cooked by her mother, she obliges us and takes us to the only restaurant in Cesarò. We do not realize yet, that Sicilians do not believe that a restaurant is better than their *mammas'* cooking. As typical Americans, we mistakenly think that going out to eat is better than going to someone's home and eating homemade authentic local Italian food. I will later learn that a meal in someone's Sicilian kitchen always tastes best, but for now we don't know any better.

Ristorante Mazzurco is not in the center of the town but on the hill that you pass when entering or leaving Cesarò. This establishment is part of a small hotel. The entire building is a renovated warehouse, formerly used by travelers with herds. The restaurant appears large and, since it is lunchtime, also busy. I notice quite a few customers in uniform. Angela informs us that these are government officials. She points out that there is only one woman among them. In Italy, the gender gap is still quite prevalent and obvious.

We are seated at a comfortable table and the ambience seems pleasant. Angela recommends some choice entrees on the menu, although we are content to have pasta pomodoro almost everywhere we go. Unlike the native Italians, we are not accustomed to eating several-course meals in the middle of the day. Angela orders *agnello*, or lamb, and I am surprised that someone so petite is able to eat so much meat at one time.

When Angela tries to explain to us what she orders, she says, "*Agnello*, the son of the sheep." She does not know the English word, lamb, and her description is accurate since a lamb is a baby sheep. Rick incorrectly thinks she is describing the testicles of a sheep, and now we really are glad that we are not choosing this entrée. Once we all believe that Angela is eating a sheep's testicles, of course none of us even want to taste any of it.

When we want to pay the bill, Angela catches us off-guard, and informs us that it is already paid, apparently by her. We are upset as our intention is to take Angela to lunch and for us to pay. She tells us sternly in English to be quiet and that is the end of the conversation. This exchange reminds me of my Grandma Savoca's sense of taking charge, as I witness an example of Sicilian determination first-hand. After this unanticipated situation, the three of us are very glad about our earlier decision to secretly leave a gift of money in an envelope in Angela's house. We assume that the salary she earns at the hotel cannot be that much and we want to show our gratitude to her.

And now the time is here to visit Angela's mother, Maria. We head over to her house. She is thrilled to see her daughter and also to meet us. Angela's father is not at home. As is his habit, he is in the countryside for a few hours. At seventy-six years old, Angela's mother is shorter than all of us and looks so cute in her red sweater and her light blonde and grey hairstyle. She immediately offers us some limoncello, which is very refreshing, and since it is home-made, how can we resist? Of course this tart, refreshing drink, which contains twenty-five percent alcohol, tastes delicious as we sip it slowly at her kitchen table and listen to Angela talk with Maria. Maria is obviously happy to spend a little time with her daughter who no longer lives at home, much to the disappointment of her parents.

A small portable TV is playing in the kitchen, but the sound does not seem to interfere with the conversation. Angela informs us later that her parents watch the news a lot, and that her father loves to watch the Weather Channel. After a while, Maria is eager to show us her home. It is very large with three floors, four bathrooms, four bedrooms, and several outdoor balconies. I have no doubt that she is extremely proud of her home, which of course is spotless. She makes sure she shows us every area including the attic, closets, basement, and garage.

According to Maria, her husband worked in Germany for thirty years before retiring, so they could buy this home. The house is seventy-three years old but does not show its age because everything is clean and well-cared for.

After our tour of the house, we walk around the corner so Maria can show us her original dwelling, the one in which Angela was born and lived until she was six years old. The home is tiny and consists of a lower room where Angela tells us the animals were kept, and later, where the children took baths in a tub. The upper level consists of the living room, bedroom, kitchen, and one toilet all in the same room. When Maria shows us the top level, we reach it by way of a pull-down door with steps. Peeking into this area we can see one room where four children and the parents slept at one time. Amazing. It is no wonder that she is so proud of her newer, much larger home where she lives now.

Quite a few situations in Sicily are so different from what we take for granted in the States. Yet, the people here are happy. Some Italians on the mainland, and particularly in the northern areas of Italy, harbor a negative view of

Sicily. At times, the mindset is that Sicily is not part of Italy. This sense of prejudice about Sicilians affects the monies appropriated for Sicily. Southern Italy, and in particular, Sicily, have very little manufacturing, so their main industries are tourism and agriculture. For these reasons, Sicilians' incomes are much lower than incomes earned in northern Italy. Government revenues are not equally distributed in the regions, one reason that the roads and transportation systems here are not up to par compared with those in Rome, Milan, Venice, and Florence.

I notice this disparity especially on the autostradas in the south, which can commonly be continuous construction sites for years at a time. Also the trains in Sicily are old rolling stock, and their routes are not comprehensive. The same holds true for the bus system, and that is why a car is really necessary to see more than a couple towns in Sicily.

My friends Angela and Teresa validate that this situation is a fact. They shrug their shoulders and say, "*Boh*," a term, which can mean any number of things, but generally it means, "So what?" or "It is what it is." They accept this as life in Sicily.

Sicily to me, though, feels like home and every person I meet extends some gesture of friendliness and help. From being invited into people's homes and offered food and drink, to the neighbors in Cesarò guiding us on the narrow streets, everyone here, so far, is accommodating.

Before saying *arrivederci* to Angela's mother, we take pictures of her and our group; then we leave Cesarò. On the way we drop Angela off at her house in Taormina. From there, Rick, Monica, and I stop for one last time on this trip at La Bussola for pizza and lemon sorbet, all for the amazing low price of eighteen euros, or a little over twenty dollars.

We say goodbye to the owners who now seem like good friends. Next, we drive back to the hotel to pack. At the reception desk, Rick leaves our request for wake-up calls at three fifteen in the morning so we can be in time at the airport.

This 2007 trip to Italy ends in Sicily, but I know I will be back to my favorite Italian region.

2009

Return to Sicily in 2009

After just two years I am eager to visit Italy again and of course Sicily. I also enjoy cruising, so after some research, I find and book a twelve-night Mediterranean cruise around Italy, with one stop in Sicily. My friend Sue agrees to go with me; she is looking forward to her first trip to the Mediterranean. At the end of the cruise our plan is to travel to Sicily for a few days because I want to see my friends Teresa and Angela in Taormina.

The cruise ship is fantastic and I am psyched about the itinerary. Royal Caribbean's *Splendor of the Seas* route has interesting ports of call, beginning with *Civitavecchia*, the nearest port to Rome. The first stop is Portofino, then Livorno for two days, and after a day at sea, a stop in Messina, Sicily. Later stops include Dubrovnik in Croatia; Venice, and Naples.

Sue and I make advance arrangements for a private excursion in Sicily with a group of other passengers from the cruise ship. The website, Cruise Critic, features a message board where cruisers can hook up with others who are traveling on the same cruise. This opportunity allows passengers to find others who are interested in the same type of excursion, and the cost is usually less than what the ship charges. Another benefit is that an excursion with a small group eliminates the distasteful feeling of being herded around like cattle.

Once the ship docks in Messina, Sue and I disembark by 8:00AM to meet our group of fourteen to go to the towns of Savoca and Taormina. "The driver is running a little late due to traffic in Messina," announces Jeff, the passenger who is responsible for pre-arranging our tour; so all is good, and we are excited.

By 8:30AM we leave the port in a large van with our driver. About an hour later we arrive in the small village of Savoca. Of course I must pose for a photo in front of the large sign that says Savoca. I do feel personally connected because of the family name. This little town's history dates back to the year 1134 and derives its name from the word *sambuchi*, Italian for elderberries.

On a side street our driver parks the van and informs us that we have an hour to explore Savoca on our own, which is fine, since the town is not that big.

Sue is experiencing Sicily for the first time. I feel excited to be with my friend as she explores my favorite foreign country. Our friendship goes back to our days as Navy nurses at Bethesda National Naval Medical Center during the Vietnam era.

My friend is eager to see the filming locations used in the Francis Ford Coppola film, *The Godfather*. We find the famous Bar Vitelli, which is not yet open at nine-thirty in the morning. As I wander through the small winding streets, I enjoy the landscape and feel as though I own the place since I do not see anyone else other than our group of fourteen. Of course, I appreciate the usual scenes of laundry hanging outside and manage to take a few photographs of one of my favorite Italian lifestyles.

A light rain is falling. "I'm glad I have an umbrella," I say to Sue.

"Me too," she says.

As we continue to explore, we encounter a priest along the road. I attempt to speak with him in Italian. "*Scusi, per favore, Padre, andiamo al Bar Vitelli.*" Excuse me, please,

Father. We are going to the Bar Vitelli." My Italian is a little better but still not that good. I hope he understands me from my recent self-study with audio CDs and some books. The kind priest indicates in Italian that he will locate the owner to open the bar for us. The *comune* of Savoca is small, so I assume that all the residents know each other.

Before he leaves to find the owner of the bar, he opens the church, *Chiesa Madre,* Mother Church. The cornerstone places the time of its construction in the fifteenth century. Beautifully decorated with white anthurium outside, the church is also adorned inside with white flowers and white ribbons. The priest explains to us that these flowers add to festive wedding rites, which take place on any day of the week in Savoca rather than just on weekends. I fully understand why this particular church is in such demand for weddings: It is absolutely beautiful with its frescoed ceiling and glass chandelier above the main altar, its stone pillars, as well as wooden pews.

The priest's friendly demeanor and winning smile makes us feel comfortable, so we stay with him at the church for a while. Eventually he drives off in his small car to find the owner of Bar Vitelli.

When Sue and I leave the church, I notice that the leaves in the anthurium arrangements outside the church doors are shaped like small vases that hold white rice. What a unique way to contain the rice to be tossed at the bride and groom for good luck after the ceremony.

By 9:45AM Bar Vitelli is open and our cruise group approaches this former movie location of the Academy Award winning film, *Godfather II*. On the outside, the bar looks the same as in the movie, complete with the same beads in shades of grey and brown hanging in front of the doorway. A lot of greenery creeps up the stone front and juts onto the roof of the building. A few small tables and chairs are situated in the open, the way I recall the scene in which Michael Corleone meets Signor Vitelli to ask for his daughter Apollonia's hand in marriage. Inside Bar Vitelli a lot of memorabilia from the movie adorn the walls, but I think it looks kind of tacky.

Inside the bar I order a cappuccino for one euro fifty cents. A lemon granita is also available here for two euros. Initially my thought is that this is limoncello, because the yellow drink looks much like it. In Sicily, as in other parts of Italy, alcoholic beverages can be a typical morning refreshment. Various liquors and wines are served in these bars, which double as cafés.

Sipping my cappuccino outside while casually browsing the small piazza, I am attracted to a small *pasticceria*, a shop which sells bakery items. Naturally I am interested and am absolutely delighted to purchase some Sicilian cookies and a pastry for an incredibly low price. My plan to save them for later quickly dissipates as I decide to eat one of the cookies while I walk around the piazza with my cappuccino. The views from here are magnificent and I can see quite a distance, even down to the sea. Two interesting sculptures command my attention on the piazza. Created by a local artist, *Nino Ucchino*, the sculptures seem to be made of a silver-colored metal, perhaps zinc, although I am not sure.

Now more of the locals begin to walk about the town and mingle in the piazza and inside the little pasticceria. The rain stops, and I strike up a conversation with an older Italian gentleman who is in the piazza. I try to explain to this man about my family name and background, and he tells me that Cesarò is about an hour away by car. I actually know this from my first visit to Cesarò as well as Savoca two years ago. Eventually this man asks me if I am *solo,* single or alone, and I think I don't really want to continue this conversation. Because I feel somewhat uncomfortable, I reply, "*Io non capisco,*" I don't understand. I find this phrase comes in handy at times in Italy.

Before we leave Savoca I purchase some stamps at the *Posta Telegrafo,* or post office, which is easy to recognize in all Italian towns by a round yellow sign with the bright blue letters, PT. As I try to speak in *italiano* with the clerks who work inside the small post office, I feel happy to be able to interact with them in this way. "*Il nome dei miei nonni è Savoca. Sono nati a Cesarò.*" My grandparents' name is Savoca and their birthplace is Cesarò. Since I am successful in having them understand me, I am pleased. This reminds me of my earlier discussion with the local priest about this same topic. What is especially interesting to me is learning that my grandfather's name is a name of nobility in this region.

Although this visit to Savoca is a short one, I love it. By 10:45AM our tour group is back in the Mercedes van and heads toward Taormina in the rain. When we arrive there, the traffic is a problem, and the driver explains to Jeff that it will take forever for him to get to the parking garage, which is up the hill. So he drops all of us off at the bottom of the hill and we take the *funivia,* or cable car, up to the top of Taormina for seven euros round-trip. I use a funivia for the first time. The views are phenomenal, although I can imagine how much better they could be in cloudless weather. The rain continues and a dense fog obscures the view considerably. Today I learn the word for rain, *pioggia*, pronounced PEE-YOE-JUH.

Once Sue and I arrive in the center of Taormina, we start walking along *Corso Umberto*, the main street in the town. We turn onto *via Luigi Pirandello*, and in no time we find a lovely pasticceria, *Bar Pirandello*. I have to wonder whether Signor Pirandello owns more than this one establishment on an entire street of the same name. The bar's green awnings have white lettering with the name of the pasticceria. The open-air tables and chairs are wet. As a rule I would choose the outdoor seating, but today it feels good to be somewhere dry and out of the rain. I am always ready to enjoy a cup of cappuccino and a cannoli. I know that the correct word is *cannolo* for a single pastry, and cannoli is the plural form, but cannoli just sounds so much better to me.

Sue and I realize that we are hungry for some lunch, so we each decide to have *panini* and Coca Light. The *panino* (panino is singular, like the cannolo) costs only two euros fifty cents, so this is a bargain, especially since we are in a resort town. We choose a table and sit down to eat, when we notice that there is no *coperto,* or cover charge. Usually in Italy there are two charges; you pay the higher one if you choose to sit down rather than stand. I am discovering that most bars in Italy do not charge a coperto, but at the same time there are no seats in many bars. We happen to be lucky here.

I order a small cannoli here too, and before we leave I notice pistachio cookies for sale here. When I inquire about these, I am told that they are made right on the premises. Without hesitation I purchase a dozen to bring home to my son, David, who loves these cookies.

Pistachios are popular in Sicily because the Sicilian town of Bronte is where the majority of pistachios are cultivated. Every other year in September the ripe green fruit is harvested. Many Sicilian desserts are made with pistachios, and they are also quite a popular ingredient in gelato. Since the area around Bronte has Arab history, it is believed that the Arab immigrants are responsible for bringing the first pistachio trees to Sicily.

When we leave Bar Pirandello, the rain lets up for a while. We return to Corso Umberto and window shop with the rest of the tourists who stroll while gazing at the many small boutiques. Since Taormina is a well-known resort city in Sicily, its main street is usually packed with quite a few travelers.

I have fun as I take photos on the street, but we duck in and out of stores to avoid the on-again, off-again rains. One establishment that piques my curiosity is a wine shop, which features *Vino alla Mandorla,* a special almond wine produced in Taormina. I purchase a couple of small bottles to take home, and so does Sue. I plan to keep one bottle for myself and give one to my younger son Brian as a gift. The three-and-a-half-ounce bottles are small enough that I do not foresee any problems of adding excess weight to the luggage, always a consideration when traveling in Italy.

The amazing church of *Santa Caterina d'Alessandria* stands in the center of Taormina, and we stop to admire its beauty. Many people are entering this seventeenth-century church, which is a magnificent example of baroque architecture. The current structure is built on the ruins of *Odeon,* and the façade is constructed with stone from the southern Sicilian city of *Siracusa*. The doors are made of marble from Taormina. Above the front entrance I see a carved statue of St. Catherine. I decide not to step inside the church; instead I shoot several photos of the church's exterior.

Sue and I keep walking leisurely along the streets of this lovely city, when suddenly I spot a truck with fresh fruit and vegetables for sale from its rear door. Again, I am fascinated and stop to capture the scene with my camera. I love the way the Italian people set up shop on a street with no apparent overhead besides a truck.

Turning off Corso Umberto we arrive at *Teatro Greco*, the Greek Theatre, one of the main attractions for tourists in Taormina. I recall the missed opportunity to visit this landmark due to lack of time two years ago. This ancient Greek amphitheatre dates back to the third century BC. The Romans rebuilt it during the second century AD. Teatro Greco prides itself as the second largest theatre in Sicily, with the largest one in Siracusa. The ancient theater still functions today as a very active entertainment stage for music, dance, and film. Each summer Taormina hosts an arts festival with many of the performances held in this theatre.

Today Sue and I have adequate time to take a self-guided tour. We pay the six euros admission price and do not yet realize that we are in for a treat. We must climb quite a few steps to reach the entrance and Sue manages to do okay, even though it is hard for her at times with her bad knees. The ruins are truly awesome; some of the original

Corinthian columns are still standing. The ancient theatre is quite large and we climb all the way up to the top tier of risers. From there we can see Mt. Etna with its snow-capped peak in the distance, just as I remember from my trip in 2007. Behind us, and over 700 feet below us, lies the azure Ionian Sea, reflecting the cloudless sky. This entire experience is indeed worth the time and effort, and my camera is working overtime.

On the walk back I suggest to Sue that we stop for something sweet to eat. "How about a cannoli and a cup of cappuccino?"

"I could go for the cappuccino and maybe a different type of pastry," Sue says. So we stop at *Bar Trinacria*, a busy bar/*gelateria*, a combination bar and gelato shop, in *Piazza Vittorio Emanuele II.* Since we do not have to meet our tour group until three o'clock, we are able take our time while we sit at an outside table and watch everyone else on the streets of Taormina. Here, for a little while, we can relate to the tradition of the sweetness of doing nothing. The Italians have a special phrase for this—*"il dolce far niente."*

Bar Trinacria's logo is the Sicilian symbol known as the *trinacria.* I notice the napkins and plates are imprinted with this symbol. Translated into English, trinacria means triangle, a name attributed to Sicily because the island is shaped like a triangle. Sicily's history includes occupation by many different nations, one reason that today food, architecture, and many traditions can be traced to ancient cultures. *Trinakrias* is the ancient Greeks' name for Sicily. *Trinacrium*, a star with three points, is the name chosen by the Romans. Today we know this Italian island in the Mediterranean as Sicily, or *Sicilia* in Italian.

At last it is time to take the funivia back down the hill. On this ride I am able to take a few photos of the coastline since the weather is improved. Our driver waits for us, and on the ride back to our cruise ship, which is docked in Messina, he makes an extra stop at the center of town so we can experience a little of this port city.

He parks the van in a large piazza where the huge Norman Cathedral is located. My research tells me that this *Chiesa della Santissima Annunziata dei Catalani* is one of the most ornamental churches in Sicily. Originally built in the twelfth century, this cathedral is the result of rebuilding after a devastating fire, several earthquakes, as well as bombings during World War II. What is amazing to me is that the repeated restorations of this magnificent cathedral result in such beauty.

The large *Piazza del Duomo* is a perfect rest stop for our group. Everyone is able to take a break and meander around the piazza, while they absorb the ambience and people-watch, one of my favorite pastimes. Many local Sicilians are in the piazza. A young boy who is playing an accordion catches my attention. Immediately I am a little suspicious and on guard, since I think he might be a gypsy. A common tactic for gypsies includes the use of children who play a musical instrument as a distraction. I scan the crowd for an adult who might be working with the child. The "worker," however, is only about six or seven years old; after a few minutes, I notice this boy make an attempt to pickpocket a few tourists. He is not successful, and, therefore, approaches some of the people and boldly asks for money. Of course, I do not pay any attention to him and walk in the opposite direction. Suddenly I see a woman sitting in a car, and I surmise she may be his mother, as I observe her watching and encouraging his behavior.

For me, the most interesting point about this piazza besides people-watching and the situation involving the gypsy boy, is the 197-foot-tall bell tower of the cathedral. At the top of this campanile is an elaborate astronomical clock with figures that perform at the top of the hour. A lion roars and a rooster crows while the figures rotate, and the clock routinely chimes. At noon this clock chimes for twelve minutes, and classical music plays. Since the time now is late afternoon, I am disappointed to be unable to witness this action. Built in 1933, this clock has more than 33,000 gears and moving parts; it boasts the distinction of being the world's largest astronomical clock, known as *Orologio Astronomico.*

One other beautiful piece of architecture in this lively piazza, to the left of the cathedral, is *Fontana di Orione*, the Fountain of Orion, a Florentine-style sixteenth-century fountain. Its pale marble construction and attention to detail in its sculptures is stunning and a good subject for some photos.

Before our group must depart, I buy a Coca Light from a vendor for one euro. Soon afterward, our driver indicates that our time here is over, and everyone returns to their seats in the van. Our group is back at the ship by the scheduled time of 5:00PM. As the *Splendor of the Seas* pulls out of the port of Messina, I can see the tall statue that sits in the half-moon-shaped harbor. This is the *Madonnina,* or Madonna statue, the protectress of the city. What a beautiful sight.

One Week Later

After a wonderful cruise all around Italy and also to Dubrovnik, Croatia, Sue and I disembark in Civitavecchia. At the port we meet another driver with whom we have a reservation. He drives us to Rome's *Aeroporto di Fiumicino*, about an hour away. From there we board a flight to Catania, the second largest city in Sicily.

My friend Angela Savoca meets us just outside the baggage claim area of *Catania Fontanarossa Airport* and I am happy to see her again after two years. "Angela, *Sono felice di vederti. Sei bellissima."* I am happy to see you. You look beautiful. After an extended hug, I introduce her to Sue. "*Questa è la mia amica, e si chiama* Sue." This is my friend who is called Sue.

"Hi, Sue." Angela smiles warmly.

Sue nods in acknowledgment. "Margie has told me so much about you. I am happy to meet you."

"Let me help you carry your luggage to my car. Then I'll drive you to our home in Taormina, where Teresa is waiting, anxious to greet you."

Shortly after we meet Angela's sister, their friend Angelica Monaco arrives. We make our introductions; everyone is laughing and talking at the same time, so happy to be together. Sue smiles but she is neither able to speak nor understand Italian. In a matter of minutes Angela, Teresa, and Angelica become very animated and I love it. We take photos and relax a bit before we all head out for dinner.

I know that Sue does not feel the closeness that I do because she does not yet know my Sicilian friends well. She feels ill at ease due to the language barrier, but she is a good sport.

"I try to go with the flow," she says.

After a while we all take off in two cars for Giardini-Naxos, where we are going to have dinner at La Bussola, our favorite seaside restaurant. Of course we have a great time with the same owner I remember from my visit two years ago, and the food is just as delicious.

Angela's English is much improved since that time, although Teresa still cannot speak or understand Sue's and my language, except for a few words and phrases. Angelica does know some English, and because of my efforts to learn conversational Italian, we can communicate much better. As in 2007, Angelica again draws the attention of the male Sicilian waiter, and the evening results in a good time.

After leaving La Bussola we drive back to the home of Angela and Teresa. Sue and I are spending the next two nights with them, thanks to their generous invitation. Since their home has three bedrooms, Angela and Teresa are sleeping in one bedroom, and Sue and I each have our own room with a twin bed in each. Such hospitality these *Sicilianos* have!

I like staying at their home because we will be able to spend more time together. After Sue and I unpack our bags, we say *buonanotte*, tired after a long but fun day.

I sleep in until seven-thirty and feel rested after an undisturbed sleep. This morning Sue awakens with a sore throat, a cough, and what appears to be the start of a cold. Teresa also complains of a sore throat, or *raffreddore*, as she calls it. Angela's throat is sore too, but I feel fine. Sue and Teresa feel the worst so they opt to stay home and rest.

So after breakfast, Angela and I take off in her car for Caltagirone, where her brother Calogero and her sister-in-law Monica LoRusso live.

Caltagirone is the Sicilian town, which is well-known for hand-painted ceramics.

Angela quickly drives to the autostrada and then heads west toward our chosen destination. The area consists mostly of rolling hills, and I see a lot of cows grazing in the fields. "*Questa è la campagna. Questa è l'unica parte della Sicilia senza montagne,*" Angela says, as she sweeps her hand from right to left. "This type of terrain in Italy is called *campagna*, which means countryside, and here you see the only area of Sicily that is not mountainous."

Along the way, located on the left side of the road, we pass Naval Air Station Sigonella, the American naval base in Sicily. It is apparent to me is that the American-style base housing looks quite out of place in Italy.

As we approach the town of Caltagirone, I feel exhilarated as soon as I can see the town perched high on a hill from a distance. An amazing view! These hilltop towns that appear after miles of countryside seem to pull me toward them. To travel in Italy and learn about its physical attractions, as well as its history, enriches my mind; but the people generate its culture. I want to meet them and learn from them.

Although I cannot find documents to verify that Angela and I are related, we are indeed close friends. And now, after two hours of driving, we finally arrive at the home of Angela's brother. Calogero Savoca is a police officer; he happens to be working in Rome right now. I am sorry that we are not able to see him this time. We find his wife, Monica, in her kitchen preparing food. She looks radiant with her striking Italian features, especially her straight coal-black hair. Her friendly smile lets me know that she is pleased we are here. She is eager to show us the home-made pasta, *tagliatelle*, and lasagna she has prepared for us. Tagliatelle are flat, ribbon-shaped strips of pasta, similar to fettuccini. Her cucina smells inviting; the air is full of the appetizing, savory aroma of freshly prepared sauce.

Since it is too early for lunch, the three of us leave the house; Monica drives to the center of Caltagirone, so we can go to a ceramics shop. "This town has hundreds of ceramic shops," Angela says, "but Calogero is friends with the owner of one particular shop, and there we have a discount—everything is half off." I am thrilled since one of my goals this trip is to purchase ceramics in Sicily, to add to my small collection at home. Receiving a discount is a big temptation.

After entering *Ceramiche Artistiche*, I cannot believe the selection and amount of items on display. This large shop appears to be organized like a bazaar where different selections of ceramic pieces are offered by different vendors, yet one woman operates the store. I am in heaven here and take my time browsing throughout the shop. In the end I line up my purchases: a biscotti jar, a clock, five Christmas balls, and three plates. While the shop operator adds up the charges, Angela points to one of the plates and gently insists, "I pay for this one. It is my gift to you." I am touched.

"*Grazie,* Angela. You are very kind and generous. Thank you."

Most of the ceramics in this shop are painted in yellows, greens, and blues. I remember hearing that each area that produces ceramics in Italy, chooses specific colors characteristic of a given town. I like these shades a lot, especially the ones with the lemon designs. At the back of the store is a large *presepe*, a Nativity scene and village, completely created from ceramic pieces. The large presepe is very detailed and is gorgeous, like nothing I recall seeing in ceramics prior to now. Monica wants to make sure that I take time to appreciate the intricate detail of this work of art here. "*Bellissima, eh?*"

"*Si,* Monica. *Bellissima,*" I say, wholeheartedly agreeing with her.

I leave this store spending only one hundred euros, thanks to Monica. The full price would definitely be over two hundred euros, and at that price would still be a good deal. At these discounted rates I am required to pay in cash. I don't have quite enough with me, so Angela pays my bill. "I'll stop at a Bancomat to withdraw euros and then repay you," I say. "It's good to have friends in Sicily. Thank you, Angela and Monica."

After our shopping expedition in this town where you cannot walk ten feet without seeing another ceramics shop, Monica and Angela want to take me to see the famous steps in the center of the town. There are 142 steps that all have unique, hand-painted ceramic tiles on the risers. No two risers are the same. This spectacular staircase is truly a work of art. It is called *La Scalinata di Santa Maria del Monte,* The Staircase of Santa Maria del Monte, the main attraction in Caltagirone.

I recall reading about this staircase but to see it first-hand is incredible. The predominant colors on the majolica ceramic tiles are sage green, yellow, and blue. They are of the same colors as most of the ceramics in the shop. The precise arrangements of potted plants and flowers on the staircase create a beautiful design. Although we do not walk up the stairs, and I am glad that nobody suggests that we do, I value the chance to take some amazing photos at the staircase, which I so enjoy. The steps lead to the upper portion of the city of Caltagirone, the location of the historic center.

After we wander around a little more in the city, we drive back to Monica's house. By this time her daughter, Martina, is home. At thirteen years old, Martina is absolutely beautiful. Her eyes are captivating; they are a strange shade between steely blue and emerald green. She appears older than thirteen, especially with the eye makeup, which accentuates her beautiful eyes even more.

She and Angela hug each other; Angela is thrilled to see her niece. "I haven't seen you for five months," says Angela in Italian, as she hugs her even tighter. Angela's present job in the hotel industry in Genoa prevents her from seeing her Sicilian family more often. She misses them. Sharing kisses, the aunt and niece delight in the reunion.

Monica immediately busies herself in her cucina where she prepares her table and invites us to sit down as she gestures to the chairs. "*Siediti qui per favore. Mangia,*" she says. Sit here please. Eat. We take our places at a table, which is now covered with platters of food: four types of cheese, two of which come from the family farm in Cesarò, and a basket of fresh bread. I am not sure who has a farm where this cheese is produced but I recall Angela mentioning some cousins with farms. The cheeses are interesting to me because three of them are types with which I am unfamiliar. I doubt that these cheeses are even available at home in the States. The cheeses are provolone, *Peraino*, smoked ricotta, and smoked ricotta with red peppers, which turns out to be my favorite. All of them are absolutely delicious. I can taste the freshness and smell the strong aroma. Monica also serves two types of olives and roasted peppers. When she sets a medium-size bowl with some colorful fruit on the table, I say. "*Che cosa è questo?*" What is this?

Monica looks surprised and says, "*Cachi, non li hai mai assaggiati?*" Cachi, you never had this?

"No. Angela, what is this in English?"

"*Non lo so. Cachi,*" Angela says. I don't know. Cachi.

This autumn fruit looks a little like a tomato but is more orange in color and tastes sweet. Later I learn that this fruit is the Italian equivalent of a persimmon. My first experience with an Italian cachi is juicy, messy, and squishy but tasty.

All this food is just the appetizer portion of the meal. We sample some of each food on the table before Monica serves the main course, which is lasagna with the homemade tagliatelle I recall seeing from earlier in the day. Each course tastes absolutely delicious and illustrates Monica's culinary skills. She seems pleased that I am enjoying the meal so much.

We finish lunch in time to take Martina to catechism class at their church. Monica is driving us a short distance farther to visit Angela's nine year-old nephew, Antonio, during a break from his school day. Although this is a Saturday, some children have school. Antonio runs outside to greet his Aunt Angela and gives her *un abbraccio*, a big hug. *"Ciao, Zia. Sono contento che sei venuto."* Ciao, Aunt. I'm glad you came.

Angela introduces us. Antonio is just darling, still very boyish but charming. He looks hip with his rectangular bright green glasses. This Savoca family is very loving and not afraid to show their affection, even in front of someone whom they don't know. I have that comfortable sense that I am at home here. I like the idea that in small communities relatives can visit the children at break time.

Monica, Angela, and I return to Monica's home where she gives me a tour. She has a huge home by Italian standards, which is tastefully decorated. The house features three bedrooms, three full-size bathrooms, a living room, two full kitchens, plus a loft with lots of storage space, which Monica calls deposit. In the loft Monica shows us a novelty item. A figure, which resembles a witch, hangs like a mobile, and when she pushes a button, the witch becomes animated and starts to make sounds. Monica seems to get quite a kick out of setting it in motion. We all laugh. I can honestly say that this is the first time I see this sort of fun item in anyone's home in Italy

At four o'clock Angela and I say goodbye to Monica. "*Grazie di tutto. La tua casa è molto bella, Monica.*" Thank you for everything. Your house is beautiful. "*Ciao, ciao.*" After a few *baci*, kisses, and hugs, Angela and I prepare to leave for her house in Taormina.

As we step outside with Monica, I notice that she has a *giardino,* or garden, which has a rosemary plant as tall as the fence. I take a moment to appreciate the woodsy fragrance of the *rosmarino*. "Mmmm, I like this."

Monica smiles and gestures toward a tree she cultivates. The healthy-looking tree is in bloom with yellow fruit, lemons. "*Limone*!" I say. "*Bellissima*."

On the drive to Taormina we have more rain, and when we get closer to Angela's home, we stop at a farmacia for Vitamin C. We also make a second stop at a *supermercato,* supermarket, for some coffee for Sue and some Coca Light for me. That evening all of us relax; at nine we have dinner together in their kitchen. The dinner consists of pasta and pizza, left over from our meal at La Bussola the previous night. It tastes delicious the second time around and is more than enough food, especially after our big lunch at Monica's house. Poor Sue is still feeling sick, and so is Teresa.

This morning I am thrilled to sleep in until eight. Daylight savings time ends this weekend and the clocks are adjusted back one hour. That extra hour of sleep last night is appreciated. Today is Sunday, and the weather is gorgeous, no rain. Teresa feels a little better but is still not fully recovered, and neither is Sue. After a breakfast of Teresa's homemade peach marmalade on bread and some Coca Light, Teresa and I walk fifteen minutes to the Catholic church. Little do we know that the usual hour-long Mass turns into an hour-and-a-half, since there is a baptism, and a new priest, according to Teresa. She is just as displeased as I am for the extra long ceremony.

Today's Mass turns out to be an educational experience for me, because the baptism is really an important event and a big deal here. Initially the baby is fully clothed, but during the baptismal ceremony all of his clothing is removed, and the priest holds him up high for the entire congregation to see. The baby boy is crying the entire time but the congregation does not seem to mind. I learn that in Sicily this ceremony is an event for all present parishioners to celebrate, not just the baby's family.

"We'll be traveling once more," I say to Sue after returning from church.

"Yes I have already packed my bags," Sue says. She feels a little better, but I can tell that she still does not feel herself. She tries to make the best of it, though. Her decision yesterday to stay home and rest, rather than go to Caltagirone, probably is the reason that she shows some improvement today. With Sue's lack of the Italian language and Teresa's minimal skills at English, conversation between the two is minimal, despite Teresa's little Italian-English dictionary. The resulting voice rest turns out to be a benefit for both of them.

Teresa serves us a wonderful lunch of *ragu*, or tomato sauce with meat in it, over homemade macaroni pasta, and it is of course quite tasty. Not being Italian and admitting to a preference for meat and potatoes over pasta, Sue does not appreciate the traditional Sicilian food as much as I do, but that is her loss. I love the meal Teresa prepares for us.

Soon Angelica stops over to say goodbye. She again looks beautiful, and we take some more photos out on the balcony with Mt. Etna in the background. Smiling as usual, Angelica is such a joy to have around and so Italian! I like her a lot and wish we had more time together. Before long, it is 4:30PM and the taxi driver arrives to take us to the airport in Catania. We need a taxi because there are three of us going, and Teresa's car is not big enough for four people plus all the luggage. Surprise! Angela is returning with us to the States. She plans to stay with me for a month's vacation. This trip is her first visit to America. I am thrilled she is coming. The price for the taxi is eighty euros and Sue and I cover the cost. "It is about an hour to Catania, so I think that's a fair price, don't you, Sue?"

"Sure. We'll split the charge fifty-fifty. How much do you think we should tip?"

"I don't know. I think eight euros is fair," I say, and Sue nods in agreement.

When we reach our destination we pay the driver and include the eight euro tip. He is gratified. In Italy tipping drivers is rare, or if patrons do it, they just add a euro or two. No wonder the non-English-speaking driver is all smiles when we pay him.

At our arrival at the airport in Catania, the desk at EasyJet is not yet open, and this begins a series of delays and chaos. During some of our waiting in line, Angela explains with a shrug that the situation is typical *italiano*. Eventually we board our flight to Milan and deplane close to 11:00PM. Since we have to be up by five-thirty in the morning tomorrow, this night at the hotel near the airport is a short one.

In the morning, Sue, Angela, and I have breakfast at the hotel. Afterward, Angela shares with me that she feels nervous and excited at the same time. Not until we are seated together on the plane, she also shares her fears, "I was not sure until this moment that I would go to America." I can tell that this decision to come with me to the States is a very big step for her. She has no idea what to expect in America. Neither of her parents knows she is accompanying me. "You mean you never told your mother and father that you are visiting America, Angela?"

"I'm almost forty years old but could not tell my parents that I'm going to America on vacation. They would have been angry and tried to stop me," she says. I am happy she is coming.

2011

Sicily in the Midst of My Solo Italy Adventure

This year my Italian solo travel plans include Venice, Udine, the hill towns of Umbria and Tuscany, and also Rome, Bologna, and many other cities on the mainland.

I like to explore the country by myself but after more than four weeks of singlehanded roaming, I am delighted that my brother Rick, and my sister-in-law Monica, join me in Milan.

"You need a day to adjust to another time zone—six hours ahead of the States' east coast time," I say.

"Yes, we'd appreciate that," Monica says.

"We could do some browsing in this city, when you two feel up to it."

"Okay, but first I want to get something to eat, and then maybe take a nap," Monica says.

"That's a plan," I say. I know that I can use this time to write while they rest for a few hours. We have two days in Milan and two days in the Cinque Terre before we head to the region of our grandparents.

Today is May 17th, the day we begin our trip together to Sicily. All three of us feel at home on that island and are eager to return, so we may discover new places, as well as revisit a few of our favorite spots. We intend to stay in Sicily for six days.

This long travel day from the Cinque Terre via Milano to Palermo culminates in frustration and aggravation. The chaotic nighttime driving situation in Palermo is more stress than any of us need. Combine that with fatigue and it makes for one of the worst days of this trip so far. By the time we finally check into our hotel at 10:30PM I am exhausted and have no problem falling asleep almost immediately.

In the morning I feel rested and approach the day with a positive outlook. I am, after all, in Sicily, and my adventure is just starting here. I hope that Monica and Rick feel the same. Now that I am no longer traveling solo, I find myself having concern over my travel companions' feelings.

We meet for breakfast in the small dining room of the hotel. "This cappuccino tastes delicious. Have some fruit, Rick," Monica says.

"I already had some," says Rick. "It felt so good to get out of that car last night. These drivers are crazy here. I can't believe there are no road signs."

"How did you sleep, Rick?" I say.

"Good. At least I feel rested. Hopefully today we can see a better side of Palermo."

"And you, Monica?" I ask.

"It felt good to sleep last night," she says. "I'm ready to walk around and see what is here."

I can tell that Rick is happy to no longer be in the stressful position of navigating around a city in the dark and not knowing where he is going. Today has to be at least more colorful.

After breakfast we head out on foot with no particular agenda. One of the first places we see is the *Teatro Massimo*, Palermo's famous opera house. The impressive domed building is a beautiful example of Sicilian baroque architecture, and Rick is the first to notice it.

"That's a famous building. I think it was in *The Godfather* movie. Remember the last scene on the front steps when they shot Michael's daughter, Mary?"

I vaguely recall that scene but I know from reading that one of the filming locations for the movie is Palermo. Now I recognize the theater, especially the massive front staircase.

"That's really neat," Monica says.

I can tell she doesn't remember the scene from the movie either. I wonder what the theater interior looks like; probably very elegant. But today we are only here for four hours, so perhaps some other time I can see the inside. For a few seconds I daydream about attending an opera one day.

As we pass by a narrow side street, *Via Orologio*, I seize a photo opportunity when I spot a vertical sign that reads *Il Siciliano*. How much more Sicilian can this be? I can already imagine a caption for this photo, which I may use in an article I write in the future. These narrow crooked streets, built for horses and foot traffic, pull at my heart and remind me of the same types of streets in Cesarò. My thoughts are once again of a time long ago, and I imagine my grandparents walking on streets like these; I feel a bit nostalgic. The connection to Sicily is strong for me. What would my Grandma Savoca think if she knew I would visit Sicily almost a hundred years after her lifetime? With a smile on my face I keep wandering these cobblestoned side streets with my brother and sister-in-law.

The noon hour approaches and as much as we wish we could linger in Palermo, we also want to move ahead and get to the warm sunny beach at Cefalù. So we return to our hotel to check out, retrieve the Peugeot, and start to drive east, with Rick behind the wheel. All of us seem to be in good moods, for which I am thankful.

On our drive to Cefalù we are able to see the Mediterranean Sea from the winding road along the northern coast of Sicily. After a quick check-in at our coastal hotel, we head to the beach to spend the entire afternoon soaking up the sun and enjoying the R&R. The water is crystal clear. "How relaxing this is. I am totally loving it and wish I could stay on this beach all day."

"I know," says Monica. "Me too."

After a few hours on this pristine beach, the three of us shower, change clothes, and then walk to the old town.

Cefalù's *centro storico* is easy to meander and I appreciate the architecture and enjoy the ambience here. I am happy wandering the narrow streets, so characteristic of Sicily. Once more I feel at home in this southern part of Italy.

Conquered by the Normans a few centuries earlier, Cefalù's architecture is a reflection of that history. In Piazza del Duomo, the giant cathedral is most famous for its amazing mosaics. After climbing the many steps leading to the Duomo, we are entering the cathedral of Cefalù. The interior is magnificent with its extremely high wooden ceilings, its marble columns, as well as its Byzantine mosaics, which are the oldest in Sicily. The focal point is the center mosaic of Christ the Pantocrator in the apse. This mosaic is larger than any of the others, and my eyes are automatically drawn to his face, full of expression, serious yet compassionate. The title of Pantocrator means Ruler of All, and this giant mosaic is a perfect depiction of such. With his right hand raised and his left hand holding the Gospel of John, Christ dominates the interior of this Duomo.

Back outside I have a chance to take in the piazza and all the activity. I always love to spend time observing the locals in an open place like this and usually find much to photograph.

What turns out to be one of my best photo opportunities is a group of elderly Sicilian men sitting on a bench. "Look at those three over there, shooting the breeze," I say to my brother. "They look like they are solving the world's problems, don't they?"

"Yeah, at their age they must have seen many changes in the world. I like how they are all wearing blue jeans," Rick says.

Monica says, "I bet they have known each other for years. They seem so comfortable together."

I enjoy watching these men as they converse with each other and laugh every so often. I record this memory forever with my zoom on my digital camera, I think about life in Sicily. This camaraderie is such an important part of Sicilian culture. I think the Sicilians are much more adept at appreciating their lives, even though each day may be simple and yet difficult at times.

After we saunter back to our beach hotel, we retire to our rooms for the night. Outside on my balcony I feel the warm breeze of the ocean against my face and smell the delicious salt air. My view of the ocean is fantastic. My day ends with one of the most gorgeous sunsets.

Rick, Monica, and I satisfy our morning appetite with yogurt, fruit, sweet rolls, and cappuccino in the hotel before we part with our beach resort. "All right, Marge and Monica," Rick says as he takes the wheel, "next stop Cesarò."

"And then on to Catania," says Monica with happy anticipation in her voice.

As we near the village I appreciate the gorgeous scenery. "Can we stop for a minute so I can take some photos, Rick?"

"Sure," he says.

Cactus grows wild along the road. From the vantage point of a high hill, we can see the entire town of Cesarò below. We can also see the Mediterranean, even though we are quite a bit inland. "Oh my God," I think to myself as I take in the panorama scene. "I am so lucky to be in such a peaceful place in Sicily." The quiet in the countryside is such a contrast to life in the bigger cities and towns. "I wonder if my grandparents ever stood in this exact spot and saw their village below the same way I see it today."

After I shoot a few photos I return to the car. "Thanks a lot, Rick. This place is beautiful and tranquil."

Once we arrive in Cesarò we drive to the home of Angela and Teresa's parents. "*Ciao, Maria. Come stai?*" I say as I greet their mother, and "*Buon giorno, signore*," as I shake hands with their father, Antonino. He seems particularly happy that we are in his home; he engages with us even though neither of us understands what the other is saying. His steely blue eyes are piercing. He wears a baseball-style cap that says Scotland and a sweater vest in shades of grey. Although Angela always tells me that her parents fight a lot, both Maria and Antonino are cordial and appear caring toward each other. After a short visit, we say goodbye and leave for Catania, our next destination. "*Grazie, dobbiamo guidare fino a Catania.*"

I would like to spend more time in Cesarò as I pass streets with names that are familiar, like *Via Secondo Scaravilli* as well as *Via Garibaldi*, which is the street listed as the place of my grandmother's birth. From what I can see, the address looks like a wall with nothing behind it, as if only the facade of the house is left.

On the way out of Cesarò we try the one restaurant in town, *Ristorante Nebrodi*, and although I can hear voices and see people inside, the doors are locked. It is two o'clock, every business is closed, and for us it is time to leave.

Catania is not one of the must-see cities for me but Monica wants to spend a few days here. "I like cities." Since this part of the trip is not just about me, Catania is on our pre-planned itinerary. I know that Rick likes being in this city because it offers opportunity to follow his passion: taking long walks. "There is so much to see," he says. So tomorrow we plan to spend the day sightseeing on foot. I may be looking for a beach after all this walking.

Breakfast in the dining room of the Grand Excelsior Hotel is like a wedding reception—the selection is endless. Different from most hotels in the U.S. is the fact that breakfast is almost always included with a reservation at an Italian hotel. When booking hotels, I always consider the savings on not having to go out and pay for breakfast.

As we leave our hotel and stroll along *Via Corso Italia* we reach V*ia Etnea*, which is a wide avenue open to foot traffic only, and a great place to take in the sights of Catania without having to dodge the ever-present Vespas.

Before too long we arrive at *Villa Bellini*, also called *Parco Bellini*, the grand park at the top of a hill. Evidently this area of green land is sort of the Central Park of Catania, and from its highest point I enjoy a panoramic view of Mt. Etna. Named after the famous nineteenth-century Catanian composer, *Vincenzo Bellini*, the park is full of exotic and ornamental plants and trees. One of the fig trees is supposedly the largest in the world, according to local Catanians.

In the garden a number of sculpted busts are on display, including one of Bellini. "Look at this," Monica says, sweeping one arm from side to side. "Who are these people?"

"I have no idea," I say, and since the inscriptions are in Italian, I do not recognize anyone famous except for Bellini. Apparently the other sculptures, which are strategically placed throughout the grounds, are of famous natives of Catania. A grand gazebo and a fountain are also focal points of interest in this combination garden and park. I like to cool off in this peaceful park and relax from the hectic city life. As we leave I notice the beverage stand located at the park entrance where one can also buy newspapers and other items. In addition, this kiosk also seems to be the hangout for some of the local police.

Further strolling takes us past the ruins of the Roman

amphitheatre at *Piazza Stesicoro*. "This looks interesting," says Rick as we stop to check the inscription at the entrance. The ancient theater, known as *Teatro Antico,* offers free tours but is only open at specific hours. At the peak of the theater's glory, the seating capacity could be up to 15,000 spectators. I find it remarkable that archeological ruins dating from the second century BC appear in the middle of a modern city.

Although the trend in writing is to use the newer terms of BCE, Before the Common Era, and CE, Common Era, rather than BC and AD, I choose to stay with the older terms because they are familiar and generally understood.

Just before we reach Piazza del Duomo we come across another church where a wedding is taking place. The entire outside area leading to the open front doors is decorated with flowers. A man is standing guard. I secretly hope to see the bride and groom but the ceremony must still be going on inside. This is the *Basilica of Santa Maria dell' Elemosina* and I later hear that this is historically the religious center for Catania's aristocratic families. No wonder that its appearance is so stately.

Piazza del Duomo is the main square in historic Catania. Large and closed to traffic, this piazza is the location of the magnificent baroque, eighteenth-century Duomo, which dominates one side of the square. The cathedral is built over the ruins of an eleventh-century church, and over the site of the original Roman baths. This elaborate cathedral is so impressive that I find myself trying to photograph it from various perspectives. Its immense size prohibits me from being able to gain a good view. I have to walk to nearly the far end of the piazza to capture it in its entirety.

Rick loves looking at all the different architectural styles and I appreciate them too, but I always prefer the activity of people watching. Just now I notice a woman wandering around the piazza holding out a cup as if begging, and she does not appear to be Italian. "Look at that woman over there, Monica. Do you think she's a gypsy?" I say.

"Yes, she looks like it to me. Maybe that's why the police are watching from across the piazza."

At one corner of the square, near the Duomo, is a heavy police presence, similar to that in Palermo. Maybe the men of the law have good reason to be watchful, although I feel safe. I am not so sure about the nighttime here, however, particularly when traveling solo.

Since Catania is a port city I am curious to see the docks; so we head in that direction. Rick and Monica are not as interested in the harbor as I am. They take a break at a little place where they order a Coca Cola Light and sit down outside for a rest. I take a walk toward the railroad tracks in the direction of the sea. Unfortunately, the tracks and a fence block me from seeing anything worthwhile of the water. All is not lost, though; I observe two separate fruit vendors and snap a few photos. Content to experience some local flavor and street culture of Catania, I walk back toward Monica and Rick, smiling. "I'm ready to join you for a cool drink," I say.

"And where should we have dinner tonight?" Rick wants to know.

"How about *Al Carpaccio*?" Monica says. "I remember the great variety of pasta and the big bowl of insalata the chef and owner served us in 2007."

One of the benefits of Catania is its proximity to the towns of Taormina and Caltagirone, where our Savoca families live. I can never come to Sicily without visiting them, so the last two days here we spend with them. Knowing them from our earlier trip makes us close. Now we can tell each other what changes affected our lives since then: Rick and Monica's new grandchildren, my granddaughters' dance and gymnastics performances, the new baby, Gioia Savoca, as well as Angela and Teresa's latest travels.

A great way to end this return to my and Rick's roots.

Arrivederci, Sicilia.

2012

Back to Sicily

Here I am: Only four months after my three-month solo adventure, I am planning another trip, and none of my friends are surprised. The allure of Italy is ever present on my mind. My initial thought is to take a transatlantic cruise. I imagine the five days at sea to be perfect for relaxing and writing, and then I also have time in Italy. I especially want to return to Sicily.

When I submit my request to schedule vacation time in May, I do not realize that the majority of spring transatlantic cruises sail in April for the repositioning of their ships. The cruise choices for May are not as comprehensive as I would like, and only one ship, Royal Caribbean's *Mariner of the Seas*, seems to be a feasible possibility The cost is, however, extremely high for repositioning cruises. Rates are usually deeply discounted to about $600 or $700 for a fifteen-day cruise, but the *Mariner* charges $2000. This ship is a great ship—I recall sailing on it during its inaugural season with my late husband—nevertheless, now it is ten years old. The high cost is not something I can afford because I will have to pay the single supplement, effectively doubling the price.

I decide to ask my friend Sue if she would like to join me again since I remember sharing the good times on our 2009 trip to Italy. At first she declines; she is about to retire, is to undergo some surgery, and is unsure of costs not covered by insurance. I am disappointed but intent on going to Italy on a cruise, especially since my vacation time is approved.

So I continue to research, this time for the Mediterranean instead of the transatlantic cruises. I need to find something more affordable since it appears that I am going.

By checking the cruise websites, I am delighted to discover a cruise on a brand new ship, which not only has a phenomenal itinerary but also features something totally unique, studio cabins for the single traveler. The *Norwegian Epic* is the first, and so far, the only ship to offer these cabins. The pricing is affordable, just slightly higher than the price of my share of a double-occupancy cabin. The more I read about it, the more I like it. So I decide to book the cruise that sails out of Rome and returns to Rome. The ports of call include Livorno, Cannes, Marseilles, Barcelona, and Naples. Barcelona in Spain and the locations in France are new territories for me to visit, thus the itinerary sounds good. It is now the middle of November, just four and a half months since my return from Italy, and I have a Mediterranean cruise booked for next May!

A few weeks later I receive a call from Sue. "Hi, Margie. Guess what? I am now able to go with you on the Italy trip."

"That's great but listen to my arrangements on the *Norwegian Epic*."

She likes what I explain to her, decides to check it out, and then books her own solo cabin. We are now going to travel together. We agree to meet up at the airport in Philadelphia and fly together to Rome. I tell her that I want to go back to visit my cousins in Colle d'Anchise again and also go to Sicily to see Teresa. We can base any other travel plans on what she would like to see since this is only her second time in Italy. I am glad to have a travel partner on this cruise. The ship sounds like a lot of fun too.

It is almost February and my months-long travel planning includes an itinerary before and after the cruise, as well as confirmed hotel reservations in Italy. Sue's eagerness to take an active part in the travel planning this time is refreshing, since two heads are always better than one. Each day I feel more excited about the upcoming trip this spring.

The message boards on the Cruise Critic website allow communication between passengers who are on the same ship. Cruise Critic has Roll Calls for each sailing of all the cruise ships. On this online forum, the passengers can contact each other and arrange for tours, excursions, and transfers to and from the port or the airport. These included services are great ways to lower the cost of some of these activities, as well as to meet fellow cruisers.

I have experience arranging a tour to the Amalfi Coast from a previous cruise, and I am doing another one this time with a family-run tour operator based in Sorrento. As an alternative to booking the ship's excursions, I can customize the agenda and tour with a small group of six or eight rather than fifty or sixty.

Sue and I coordinate an itinerary and decide to spend a few days in Lake Como and then Verona before the cruise.

We make arrangements to rent a car in Rome at the end of the cruise. The plan is to drive to Colle d'Anchise, then on to Sicily before heading back to Rome. We can share the driving so it will not be too stressful. The cost of gas is high everywhere, and in Italy today the price of one liter hit 1.96 euros.

If I do my math correctly, a liter is just a little over one fourth of a gallon, so it takes approximately four liters to equal a gallon. One gallon of gas in Italy then is approximately four times today's price of one liter, or close to eight euros. At today's exchange rate of 1€= $1.31, one gallon of gas in Italy would cost close to $10.50. This makes today's price of $3.80 a gallon in the States a bargain. Everything is relative, though, because Italians drive less and walk more than Americans do, and most likely do not have the long commutes to work so commonly found in the States.

Since our plans call for us to rent a car in Rome, drive to Sicily and back to Rome (I know, call me crazy), I guess I need to plan on a few hundred more euros to cover the gasoline costs. Supposedly the car is a Fiat 500 and at least the gas mileage of those cars is good, somewhere between 33 and 38 mpg. We'll see.

I am signed up for a Conversational Italian course with Lori, my teacher. So far the classes prove to be a good challenge for me, because the other three students are all better at Italian than I am, and I have to really put forth an effort to keep up. For an hour and a half the students mostly converse in Italian and read a little for pronunciation and comprehension. I really need the practice so that I can still communicate in Italian when I go back to Italy in a few months.

For the fifth time this year Mt. Etna is erupting again in Sicily, spewing lava and ash into the neighboring towns. Although Etna is one of the places on our agenda to visit next month, I am beginning to question whether it is a good choice or not. In an e-mail to Sue I say. "Are you sure you want to go there? I think God is telling us something here, maybe. We may have to play things by ear. At least no plans are written in stone and flexibility is the name of the game when traveling to Italy, and especially Sicily."

At this point I am leaning toward skipping an excursion to the active volcano and exploring another part of Sicily instead. I think my friend and travel partner is still interested in going to Etna. *Vediamo.* We'll see.

Now, just a few weeks later, Mt. Etna erupts again, and if you're keeping track, this is the seventh time this year and the third time this month. One week from today I depart for Italy and still plan to go to Mt. Etna during my visit there. I think it would be fantastic to see it erupting from a distance.

Yes, our trip is only a week away and I feel the excitement, although I am still not packed. As I pay attention to the weather reports, I try to decide if I need clothes for warm weather or cool weather, and I guess I need both. Since I remember how difficult it is to lug bags onto trains and up and down staircases, I try to pack lightly. Always a challenge for me, no matter how many times I go somewhere or for how long unless it is just for a day or two. It seems I always have something to sew at the last minute too. I can never understand how people can pack for a long trip in an hour or less.

"All my bags are packed, I'm ready to go." Just a few more days now until "I'm leaving on a jet plane," although unlike John Denver's lyrics, I do know when I'll be back again. Sue and I land in the Eternal City Thursday morning, but there is no sightseeing in Rome for these travelers because we plan to catch the Leonardo Express train from inside the airport.

A thirty-minute ride is expected to take us to Rome's main train station, the Termini; from there Sue and I intend to board a fast train to Milan, to ride another train for an hour to Varenna, and to follow that up with a short walk to the ferry to transport us across Lake Como to the beautiful resort town of *Bellagio*.

Aah, to have three days to enjoy once again the beauty and tranquility of Lake Como. Sue looks forward to staying there after hearing my stories. You can be sure that I intend to keep my eye open for George Clooney too, since he frequently spends time at his Lake Como villa in the warmer months.

With that agenda I won't have to worry trying to stay awake to overcome the time difference quickly. Out of necessity I am forced to stay up and the jet lag should not impact me for too long. When I travel from the U.S. to Italy, I believe that the best way to handle the jet lag is to stay up all day when I first arrive. Flights from the U.S. typically arrive in Italy in the morning, which really is about 3:00AM U.S. time. So if I am able to sleep on the plane, and then stay up all day until at least eight or nine in the evening Italy time, I am good to go.

Leaving for Italy

The day I leave for Italy, May 2nd, is finally here. I board my flight from West Palm twenty minutes later than scheduled, and the plane takes off at 2:15PM. I should land in Philadelphia in about an hour and a half, and from there leave for Rome. Awake until almost three this morning I hope to be able to sleep on the overnight transatlantic flight to Rome.

On the flight from West Palm to Philly, I am seated next to a US Airlines flight attendant. Near the end of the flight we start a conversation. Since he is in uniform I am curious about his schedule. "I am off duty now and will stay overnight in Philadelphia before my next assignment begins tomorrow. When we land I'm going to see if I can pull some strings for your transatlantic flight. I won't promise anything but I'll try."

"Thank you so much, Daniel. I really appreciate that. It has been a pleasure meeting you. Thanks again." I do not know what he can possibly do although I appreciate the gesture. My last check of the seating chart on Delta's website shows that the flight to Rome is full, so I am not anticipating any special favors.

After this plane touches down in Philadelphia, I am eager to disembark. Once inside the airport I quickly navigate the concourse to the gate where I expect to meet Sue for our flight together to Rome. From a few hundred feet away I see her sitting in the waiting area and feel the excitement. "Hi, Sue. I'm so glad to see you. How was your flight?"

We hug each other and, smiling, Sue says, "Good, Marge. I can't believe we're here."

"I know. I'm really excited. I know we will have a great time." We do not have long to wait before the agents announce that the boarding process is about to begin. Sue and I know that we are not seated near each other. After I locate my seat, I notice that the one next to me is empty— for a few minutes I think that maybe Daniel somehow is able to have some input. Maybe I am going to have the benefit of more room, I think to myself. No such luck — a woman shows up at the last minute, just before the doors of the plane close, and the empty seat next to me is now history.

After about a half hour into the flight an Italian gentleman seated behind me kindly switches seats with this woman so that she and her husband can sit together, and now this Italian man will be sitting to my left for the duration of this flight. I look at this as a good opportunity to practice my Italian. It turns out that Romano speaks both his and my native languages exceptionally well because his birthplace is Rome. At the age of sixteen he moved to Philadelphia. Later he returned to Rome, where he lives now. Romano is extremely pleasant and a true gentleman. He looks like an Italian version of an older Richard Gere. Very easy on the eyes.

The long flight passes quickly as we chat for the first half of the trip. "*Piacere di conoscerla*," he teaches me. Nice to meet you. An easy phrase to memorize, I foresee adding it to my Italian conversations. *Grazie, Romano.*

I only sleep in bits and pieces, like catnaps, but when the plane lands just before 9:00AM Italian time, I actually feel rested. After Sue and I retrieve our bags, we find a Bancomat, withdraw some euros, and then head to the train station inside the airport. Here we each purchase a ticket for fourteen euros to take the Leonardo Express nonstop train to Rome's Termini. Once we arrive at the central station we have an hour to wait until our train to Milano leaves. "Do you want to get something to drink and sit down before our train comes?" Sue asks.

"Sure, I think I saw a place over there. Let's check it out," I say. Sue and I each order a beverage and discuss our strategy for our next adventure. "Since our train has already arrived and is sitting on the track, why don't we board early, as soon as they open the doors, so we have time to find spots for our luggage?"

"Okay, good idea, especially since my bag is so big," says Sue.

For me the biggest challenge of train travel in Italy is finding a spot for the luggage. I like to place my bag where I can see it; sometimes it fits between seats, and other times there are spots at the end of each car. Even though I have a medium-size bag, the weight between thirty-five and forty pounds makes it difficult for me to lift it over my head. Sue, on the other hand, has a much larger bag, so it is even more of a problem for her to find a spot. Some kind, younger passengers offer to help her. Then we take our seats. It never fails in Italy that someone will offer you help. "*Vuoi una mano?*" Do you want a hand? Sometimes I do not understand the question clearly, since Italians speak rapidly. By now I am used to hearing it and am always grateful for the offer.

After our train reaches Milano's Centrale we grab a quick bite to eat inside the station and catch the regional train to Varenna. The train is full so I am standing in the area between the cars where I can keep an eye on the luggage.

"*Ciao, lei parla inglese?*" I say to the young man facing me.

"*No, Italiano,*" he says. When I realize that he speaks zero English, I seize the opportunity to speak Italian and enjoy the exchange.

"*Sono Americana. Ho studiato l'italiano per due anni.*" I am American and I studied Italian for two years.

"*Brava.*" Good.

"*Grazie.*" I guess I still remember a lot of my Italian! That conversational Italian class is definitely paying off for me.

For the next ten days Sue and I travel about in mainland

Italy, spending three wonderful days in Bellagio, then going to Verona for two days, and then back to Rome where we leave from the port of Civitavecchia for a seven-day-cruise on the *Norwegian Epic*. We love the ship and really like the ports of call despite Sue's setback after a fall on a back street in Verona, and yet another fall on the ship, which results in an injured arm. Both of us are nurses and neither of us thinks that her arm is broken. Later, however, after Sue returns home and seeks medical attention, she is told that she has indeed a fractured arm.

After our seven-night Mediterranean cruise, we are now back at the port of Civitavecchia, where the disembarkation process this morning is seamless. By 8:00AM Sue and I are on the dock waiting for the rest of our pre-arranged group to meet the driver assigned to take us to the airport. There the two of us pick up a rental car, supposedly a Fiat 500 with automatic transmission. Like many situations in Italy, arranging a rental car is not free of problems. The following event depicts a not unusual predicament in Italy, where a certain amount of patience is required if you intend to rent a car here.

By nine thirty Sue and I are at the rental car desk at *Fiumicino* Airport. After taking a number, it is another forty-five minute wait before we speak to a person at the desk. A minor fiasco develops when the agent informs me that she does not have a record of the reservation. "No voucher," she says in English.

"What?" I say, irritated. "I have a reservation."

"But you need a voucher." She tells me to wait. After several phone calls in Italian and many more time lapses, we eventually have the keys to a Mercedes Class A mid-size car. Our choice is either that or a Smart car, since they do not have the Fiat 500, of course, and a Smart car is way too small.

Slightly annoyed, we depart from the rental car desk but fail to take the ticket that is needed to get out of the parking lot. Now I am dealing with even more delays since the gate does not open for me to drive out of the parking area. I have no other option except to turn the car around and walk back inside to find the self-service machine and obtain the ticket that will allow me to exit the parking lot. At noon I drive out of Rome. Our original plan to share the driving is changed because of Sue's injury. With the pain and limited movement she feels in her arm, she does not know if she can drive. We decide to play things by ear and I drive for now.

This is my first experience driving in Italy; thank goodness we have a GPS. Eventually we are on our way to the region of *Isernia*, where we plan to stop at the small village of *Longano*. I like this town that bears my maiden name, Longano.

"So, during the next twenty-four hours this Mercedes will take us to Longano and then to *Colle d'Anchise*, where Antonella Baratta and her family live," I say to Sue.

"You have told me about them. Antonella is your cousin, isn't she?"

"Yes," I say. "She's my fourth cousin on my father's side of the family. First, though, let's check in at *La Piano dei Mulini*, our accommodations for tonight."

La Piano dei Mulini is an *albergo diffuso*, which is similar to an agriturismo or farmhouse, and functions as a hotel. It is a fine, relaxing place to stay; this is my third time here. Sue wants to rest while I visit with my cousin and her family for a couple of hours. Afterward, I return to meet Sue for dinner at the restaurant at La Piano dei Mulini.

The following morning we are on our way to Sicily by way of the autostrada, the A3, which is under construction all the way to Sicily. Not only that, but we experience a one-hour delay due to a detour through the mountains, as well as a forced backup of traffic due to a disabled truck stopped along the highway. To say the situation is frustrating is an understatement. The roads and infrastructure of southern Italy are definitely not what they are in the northern sections of the country.

To make up for my exasperation, I take pleasure in seeing the beautiful, mountainous landscape which surrounds me. At this time of year the scenery is very green. On either side of the road farms appear here and there and an occasional hillside town appears in the distance. As we travel through the regions of *Basilicata* and *Calabria*, individual houses dot the countryside. No big cities are anywhere close to our driving route.

I like seeing the goats and sheep grazing, although I never actually know if these animals are goats or sheep. Later I learn a tip to identify them as simple as looking at their tails. Goat tails point upward and sheep tails hang down. Another clue that we are in the campagna are the numerous road signs warning of cow crossings although I do not see any cows.

Sue is not feeling well; she is coughing a lot, so she is not too talkative. "I'm sorry you are sick. I wish I could do something for you," I say.

"Thanks. I hate being sick on vacation."

"I know. I hope you start to feel better soon."

"I wish I could help drive, but I just don't trust this arm. It keeps catching." By mutual decision I am doing all the driving. We want to be on the safe side since Sue does not trust her arm at this point. The only downside to this idea is that Sue as a passenger is somewhat nervous and acts like a backseat driver. However, I am aware of her tendency, so things are okay.

Once we reach *Reggio Calabria* the terrain changes, and we take in the incredible views of the blue water and the beaches below. I so appreciate the GPS because its voice directions guide us directly to the ferry crossing in the town of *Villa san Giovanni*, the last town in Reggio Calabria before crossing into Messina. The car ferry costs forty euros for a round trip, not a bad deal since a one-way ticket costs thirty-three euros. Our intent is to drive back across in a few days, so we opt for the round trip ticket. Of course we have to wait for the ferry to load, which involves another hour. MapQuest does not calculate this added time.

Hello Again, Sicily

Leaving Colle d'Anchise at ten thirty this morning, we arrive tired at our accommodation in *Milazzo*, Sicily at nine in the evening. After driving all day from Rome to Sicily, I doubt that I will drive to Sicily ever again. This is an exceptionally long day and the drivers in Messina are the absolute worst. They park their vehicles anywhere, including the driving lanes and crosswalks. I feel fortunate to arrive here without incident. Moreover, the cost of diesel fuel here is €1.73 a liter. Flying to Sicily may be a wiser and less expensive option in the future.

After the luxury of a cruise, staying in hotels for one night at a time is not so appealing and probably not the best idea. Note to self for future trips: Plan better on this detail. The hotel in Milazzo is much less than desired; in fact it is terrible.

Instead of the location being on a beach as anticipated

when booking the reservation, I discover that the hotel is instead situated on a dock in an industrial area. With absolutely no view, the room has a sliding door that opens onto an open terrace with extremely high walls. Other rooms also open onto this same terraced area, so there is no privacy. I do not plan to ever stay in this Hotel La Bussola again and in fact not in Milazzo either. (I think it ironic that a hotel that is so unpleasant has the same name as a restaurant that is so appealing.).

Later, as I tell this story to my Sicilian friends, all of them indicate that Milazzo is *brutto,* ugly, and in no way compares to the many other beautiful seaside places in Sicily. Cefalù it is not. I gather that all seaside locations are not the same and not necessarily beautiful either just because they are on the water.

I must say that the hotel is at least clean and modern, and the front desk staff personnel are very pleasant. The reason for choosing this particular hotel is its proximity to the ferry in the port of Messina: only forty-five minutes by car. Both Sue and I are grateful for a shower and a good night's rest in clean beds.

Now that we are rested, we are planning our day. Our original plan is to drive to Mt. Etna this morning and to my friend Teresa's in Taormina in the afternoon. During a phone call to Teresa, however, she informs me that Etna is too far and will take much more time than I realize. "*No Etna...troppo lontano*," Teresa says. The arrangements with Teresa involve meeting her after she finishes work at 1:00PM, so the timing is very tight.

Seeing Mt. Etna is the one thing Sue cares about in Sicily. She is not happy that we are not going there. Her arm hurts and she still has a cough. "I just want to rest. Take me to a hotel and I'll just rest there and you can go to Teresa's." I don't know if she is just upset about not having time to go to Mt. Etna, or if she would rather rest because she doesn't feel well. The option of getting up really early and trying to go to Mt. Etna is no longer a possibility since it is now mid-morning.

Sue's preference to stay in a hotel rather than stay with Teresa is not a surprise because I am aware that she feels more comfortable in a hotel, and I am fine with that. "Okay, let's find a nice hotel in Taormina," I say. Consulting the internet we find a hotel that seems comfortable for a reasonable price, so we make a reservation online. After checking out of this awful hotel in

Milazzo we drive to Taormina without much conversation; things seem pretty tense between us. The hotel in Taormina looks beautiful and I help Sue carry her bags inside and check in. Then I continue to Teresa's house with the agreement to pick Sue up in the morning. Although I feel badly about the fact that Sue is not able to go to Mt. Etna, I am happy that I can spend the day with Teresa. Sue's decision not to accompany me to Teresa's is probably best. She does not seem to enjoy being around Italians because she cannot communicate with them. It is what it is, I am thinking, and I am looking forward to being with my Sicilian friend whom I consider family.

Shortly after arriving at Teresa's house, I get settled and freshened up."Would you like to go to Caltagirone to visit my brother and his family?" Teresa says.

"Yes. And later could we visit Siracusa too?"

"No, there is not enough time," Teresa figures.

Intentions always take so much longer in reality than they do in planning. It pays to be flexible. I make a note to visit Siracusa another time. Teresa and I drive to Catania to pick up her brother Calogero after work. I appreciate his help in retrieving my misplaced passport last year, so I am eager to see him and his family again.

What irony: On the way to Caltagirone we can see Mt. Etna. Smoke is escaping from its peak. "*Vediamo il fumo ogni giorno da quando c'e` stata l'eruzione il mese scorso*," Teresa says. Such an unusual sight. The other side of the volcano has snow on it! As though she reads my mind, Teresa stops the car so I can take a photo.

I don't dare share this opportunity with Sue, whose disappointment at not seeing Mt. Etna is a nagging source of tension between us. I sense the friction, because, as stated before, Sue and I have different priorities for our visit to Sicily. But due to her painful arm and bad cough, the Mt. Etna agenda is not happening. I hope that after a good night's rest in the hotel by herself, she and I can smooth things over.

Once Teresa and I arrive in Catania, we wait for Calogero at the police station. "I see him," I say. Teresa switches over to the passenger seat of the car. As Calogero approaches the car, he recognizes us, waves, and says, "*Ciao*," with a smile, and Calogero assumes the role of driver when he joins us.

On the way to Caltagirone, he makes a stop to purchase some fresh *ciliegie*, cherries, and when we reach his home, his wife, Monica, is waiting for us with a warm welcome. I am thrilled to see Martina and Antonio again. "*Ciao, Monica. Sono così felice di vederti! Ciao, Martina* and *Antonio.*" I am so glad to see you. Plenty of hugging and smiling makes me feel once more like I belong here. We are, after all, Savocas. I love this Italian family of mine in Sicily.

After a while Teresa, Calogero, Monica, Antonio, and I drive to the center of town to look again at the famous ceramic staircase with all the flowers on the 142 steps. Martina drives on her own since she is a teenager with a scooter. Although this is my third visit here, it is my first experience of climbing the steps—we are all walking the stairs together. What I find intriguing are the many small shops, tucked into little alleys at different levels along the staircase. Not surprisingly many of these shops feature hand-painted ceramics. At the top of the staircase is the eighteenth-century *Chiesa di Santa Maria della Monte.* When we enter this sacred place of worship, my eyes are immediately drawn to the chandelier. This stunning work of art appears to me to be Murano glass with its clear, white glass candles, accented with lavender and pale blue glass flowers. Truly one of a kind.

The historic center of Caltagirone is at the top of the steps, where we explore the area and I take many photos. I notice how old some of the doors and alleys are. I always like wandering in the centro storico of a town, especially when the alleys are narrow and winding as they are here. One staircase is so narrow that I can touch both side walls. Also interesting are the many shrines embedded into the stone walls here. Most seem to be to the Blessed Mother. One of them on *Via San Giuseppe* is of the Holy Family; it is framed with turquoise and purple ceramic, pyramidal-shaped tiles, which not only surround the rectangular frame but continue the design to make the frame look like a church with a cross above. A small padlock secures the picture beneath a sheet of glass.

We retrace our steps back to the chiesa, take some family photos, and walk back down La Scalinetta. In the piazza below we meet up with Martina, who is with her teenage friends. She seems to have a new friend in the form of a puppy. She cradles this tiny animal in her arms and wears a big smile. After some conversation we separate and Martina continues to hang out with the teens. The rest of the Savoca family and I continue to meander the streets of Caltagirone.

With no agenda and in no particular hurry we browse the shops and come upon an art gallery where several young artists are working. This gallery space is the first of its kind here and one of the artists, *Miriam Pace*, kindly shows us around the work space. She speaks English and proudly says, "Next year I will come to New York and exhibit my paintings at an art expo, I hope."

One of the other artists, *Santy Ufo*, is re-creating miniature ceramic pieces to look like the originals, damaged some time ago. "*Che bello*," how beautiful, I say to Santy. Pleased that I like his work, he takes time to show me some of the pieces he is painting and describes them in Italian. I feel honored to meet these dedicated artists in this artistic town.

I love being with the family today and speaking Italian with them all day. Teresa is studying English and understands a lot more English than a year ago. Martina and Antonio know a few words, as does Calogero, but basically the conversation is in Italian, which is good practice for me. Sue would not enjoy this day; she would feel uncomfortable being around local Italians and not be able to participate in the conversation. For me though, this family time today is my favorite part of being in Sicily.

I love watching Antonio, almost fourteen, as he walks arm in arm with his dad in the streets. This scene is not one commonly seen in America, which is why I appreciate its meaning. When we return to Calogero and Monica's house, it is almost eight thirty. My original plan to drive back and then take Teresa out to dinner changes once she checks her watch and tells me that by the time we return to Taormina it will be too late. No problem. Within a few minutes Monica whips up an amazing dinner of pork filets, artichoke *frittata*, omelets, salad, some salami and prosciutto, fresh cheeses, bread, as well as pastry filled with *nutella*, the popular Italian hazelnut chocolate spread. Without being asked, Martina helps set the table and brings out some of the food from the refrigerator. "Can I help?" I ask.

"No, no, sit here," says Martina, and within minutes Monica serves a meal better than we could have in any restaurant. She is an awesome cook; everything she prepares is always delectable.

An hour and a half later, Teresa and I say goodbye and drive back to her house. We arrive by eleven, very tired, after a marvelous day in Sicily.

Aware that I only have a few hours left in Sicily, I need to do one last thing before I say goodbye to Teresa this morning. "I'll be back in a little while, Teresa," I say. After she unlocks the door for me, I walk the short distance to *Caffé Augusto*, the pasticceria where I remember having delicious cannoli and cappuccino last year with my sister-in-law Monica.

"*Buon giorno. Vorrei due cannoli e alcuni biscotti, per favore*," I say to the young woman behind the counter. Good morning. I would like two cannoli and some cookies, please. I buy an assortment of Italian cookies for Teresa to say thank you for her hospitality.

"*Arrivederci, Teresa. Ti voglio bene. Grazie mille. La prossima volta tu vieni a casa mia.*" I love you. Thank you so much. Next time you come to my house. Goodbye, Teresa.

After a hug and two kisses I am on the road by a quarter past eight. I need gas, so I make a stop and pay over nine dollars a gallon. Because I cannot figure out how these gas pumps work here, I opt for full-service. An attendant happily fills my tank for me, and I am grateful for the service. With the gas gauge on full, I head toward Sue's hotel at the upper part of Taormina to retrieve my travel partner. Driving in the touristy upper section of Taormina is challenging, and finding a parking spot is even more of a process. I am glad I arrive early since I end up parking approximately a quarter of a mile away from the hotel, down a hill, of course.

By a quarter past nine I pick up a well-rested but quiet Sue, and we are on our way back to the mainland of Italy. We must cross the strait of Messina again on the ferry, and I calculate our trip to be a five-hour drive, barring any detours. Well, we encounter plenty of delays, and the first one involves locating the ferry dock. Apparently two different ferry companies operate on two separate docks, and the GPS directs us to the wrong one.

Now we are armed only with directions we receive in Italian from the man at the dock.

"Do you understand what he said?" asks a nervous Sue.

"Some of it," I say. "I hope we can figure it out. The other dock can't be too far from here."

After about a half hour of being lost, we eventually locate the right place and drive the car onto the ferry. "Finally," I say. "This is unbelievable."

"I know. I can't wait to get out of Sicily," Sue says.

"At this point, neither can I," I admit "The driving has been crazy here."

As the ferry sails away from Sicily I see Mt. Etna in the distance with smoke still coming out of it. I don't even mention it to Sue, afraid of stirring up yesterday's disappointment. After about twenty-five minutes we cross over into Reggio Calabria, where we drive in the direction of the autostrada. Prior to actually getting onto the autostrada, we are forced to take yet another detour of non-highway roads for another hour. I am convinced that nothing happens fast in Italy, and life moves even slower in southern Italy.

One other small curveball to this travel day is a traffic stop by the Italian police. I assume the reason the police officer is stopping me is due to the slow-moving car in front of me. He motions for me to pull over and the other car is also now on the side of the road. When the Italian-speaking police officer asks to see my *documenti*, documents, I hand him my passport, driver's license, and international driver's license, hoping this will be enough. I am thankful I have all these documents with me but still have no clue as to why I am here. "*La turista?*"

"*Si, sono Americana*," I say to him. Once he realizes that I am a tourist, he continues to speak in Italian although I do not quite understand all of it. So he resorts to hand gestures and indicates that no passing is allowed when a yellow line is in the road. Now I should know this since the same rule applies in the States, but for some reason in Italy I guess my mind is not completely in gear. I know he is right, and I remember passing the other car even with the yellow line. Suddenly it dawns on me that I am definitely at fault. Oh no, I wonder what will happen now, I think. A quick visual of an Italian police station or worse, yet, Italian jail, crosses my mind. Will he write me a ticket? Will I have to go to *la polizia*, police station?

Fortunately for me, this officer kindly lets me go with a warning, as he hands me my documents."Goodbye," he says with a smile. I think he wants me to know that he speaks some English, and I smile back.

"*Grazie mille*. Thank you." This is definitely your lucky day, Margie, since you are the one who is actually in violation of the driving laws in Italy.

A trip that in essence should take six hours ends up taking ten. And I can say that I now have the longest continuous driving experience behind me after forty-five years of driving. Just before dark, Sue and I arrive tired and hungry at *Hotel Olimpico* in *Pontecagnano*, not far from the Amalfi Coast and Salerno. The hotel staff are extremely accommodating and very pleasant. This hotel is a family-run business and the front desk personnel speak excellent English as well as Italian. The hotel is a welcome sight— absolutely beautiful.

Hotel Olimpico's restaurant is open until 10:00PM. After we check in at the reception desk, we take a little time to freshen up after our travel day. But before we head to the restaurant, I initiate a conversation with Sue about the tension between us for the past two days. She tells me that between her arm hurting and having a cough, she is ready to go home.

"I had a good time on the trip, but not in Sicily, and yes, I was disappointed about missing Mt. Etna. I didn't pursue it further with you, because you wanted to be at Teresa's by the early afternoon."

I want to smooth things over between us and apologize for any miscommunication on my part. So I suggest we make the best of it and enjoy the last day and a half here. We talk about an agenda and decide together to go to

Maiori tomorrow and spend some leisure time along the beach there.

"I think you'll like Maiori, Sue. The beach is beautiful and we can sit outside and relax there." I am grateful we have this conversation after the stressful past two days. Things seem better between us and we go to dinner.

Tonight feels a little too cool to eat outside but the indoor restaurant is lovely. A friendly elderly Italian man named Giuseppe, with a nickname of *Peppino*, is our waiter. After a glass of wine for me and a Pina Colada for Sue, we both begin to unwind and are able to relax at last. Sue orders lasagna and I choose pasta pomodoro. But then I think about *cotoletta alla Milanese*, breaded veal cutlet, although I do not find it on the menu. "*Per favore, signore, è possibile avere una cotoletta?*" Is it possible to make cotoletta?

Peppino smiles and nods. "*Si, desidera una cotoletta? La prepariamo per voi.*" Yes, you want cotoletta? We will make it for you.

"*Grazie, signore.*" When he brings my order to the table I am not disappointed. It looks well prepared and is so delicious that I surprise myself by being able to eat everything. After dinner Sue and I call it a night and neither of us has any problems sleeping in our luxurious accommodations. I feel much better now that the tension between us is gone.

The following morning Peppino is on duty again in the breakfast room and greets us with his smiling face. He truly looks and acts as if he totally enjoys his job here. He is holding a frying pan with five sunny-side-up eggs, decorated with three small tomatoes and a sprig of fresh basil in the middle. Breakfast at Hotel Olimpico is a huge buffet with everything you can imagine. Just the selection of fresh fruit is astonishing with cherries, strawberries, kiwi, pears, apples, peaches, persimmons, watermelon, and cantaloupe.

It is a gorgeous morning. Sue and I opt to eat outside on one of the terraces and enjoy the ambience. After such rough travel yesterday it feels so good to be able to take our time here and just derive pleasure from our surroundings. The grounds are perfectly manicured and landscaped; they could be a magazine feature. I wish our stay were not just the one night. There is a private beach just across the street and I cannot believe all the amenities that come with the price of a reservation. The tennis courts as well as bocce courts are free to use by the guests. The hotel provides also a complimentary shuttle service to Salerno and other locations on the Amalfi Coast.

This morning I have the pleasure of meeting *Gaetano*, who is one of the young owners. When I mention that we are driving to the Amalfi Coast and then on to Rome, he provides us with a map and detailed instructions to get to the Amalfi Coast road by bypassing Salerno. "Today there is a race, a marathon, in Salerno, and the main roads will be closed," he says. "You must go a different way to Amalfi. I will show you how to go." Thank goodness he shares this information with us; without that I can only imagine another series of delays.

He also says that the autostrada from Sicily to Salerno is the worst one in Italy and is always under construction. He explains further that the one between here and Rome is a much better highway, in fact the best in Italy. So at least this is something to look forward to for our last day of driving in Italy. Before we leave, Gaetano presents me with a small wrapped gift and tells me it is from *Vietri sul Mare*. I am touched. "That is so nice of you, Gaetano. I know that Vietri is known for its hand-painted ceramics and I really appreciate this. *Grazie mille*, Gaetano."

"My pleasure, and we hope you will return here soon." I am thinking that I hope so too, and wonder when that might be.

Gaetano's directions to the Amalfi Coast road turn out to be perfect and as long as I keep following signs for *Costiera Amalfitana*, or Amalfi Coast, I am in the right spot. Only once do I end up going the wrong way on a one way road, and since there is not too much traffic I am able to correct this without any problem. One other small glitch is a wrong turn, which forces us to drive uphill a few miles into another town. The payoff is the scenic view from there. After I pay the same toll twice, I manage to find my way back to the Amalfi Coast road below.

I recall this stretch of the Amalfi Coast from riding on a bus last year, so I know what to expect, although the trip seems longer now that I am the one driving. Because there is not much traffic, I can take my time and drive leisurely without feeling rushed. This meets with Sue's approval too, because she is nervous in the front seat on these winding narrow roads. The multiple S-bends and switchbacks on this road trigger my memories of the mountain roads in the western United States and through some of the national parks in California.

The Amalfi Coast is just stunning with its high cliffs and rock formations all the way down to the sea. I think this has to be my favorite spot in Italy. We pass the little town of Vietri sul Mare, and I am able to find a spot to pull over and capture a photo of this beautiful place. Known also as the "First Pearl of the Amalfi," Vietri sul Mare is the first town on the Amalfi Coast, or the last, depending on which direction you drive. Then we pass through the little fishing village of *Cetara*, a town I remember from one of the television travel shows. I consider making a stop here but instead decide to go to Maiori since I am familiar with it, and I know that there is a nice promenade along the beach, as well as a place to park. Here in Cetara I am not about to practice parallel parking on these winding and steep roads.

Maiori is so beautiful. I will never forget five glorious days from last year in a Franciscan monastery in a room with a view of the ocean. A gentle breeze is ever-present, and although today is cloudy, I still feel wonderful being at the ocean. Once we park the car, Sue and I cross the street and walk a little along the promenade. Then we sit down at the outdoor beach bar, *Lido La Bussola*, and order several cappuccinos. Both of us love being near the water, and I think that this is the perfect antidote to the tension from yesterday. As much as I love Sicily, I find the tranquility of this coast almost mesmerizing. I am so happy to be here. Sue seems happier too, so all is good. The atmosphere here is perfect for relaxing, and Antonio is very happy to sell us cappuccino for only one euro fifty cents a cup.

I walk across the street and buy a gelato which is another bargain, two scoops for two euros. I have pistachio and *amarena,* made with Italian-grown amarena cherries. I realize that this will likely be my last gelato in Italy before I fly home tomorrow, so I am savoring every bite. Once I am back at Lido La Bussola, Sue and I sit for a while longer, and appreciate being in this idyllic setting without an agenda. "Isn't this nice?"

"Beautiful," Sue agrees. It is only two or three hours to Rome and we have all day to get there.

We leisurely walk along the promenade again before leaving Maiori, and suddenly Antonio comes running down, calling after us. "*Signora, signora.*" He is waving something in the air, and when Sue sees him, she realizes that he has her wallet. "I must have left it on the table when we had the cappuccino," she says. "*Grazie.*" How nice of Antonio to run after us to return her wallet. Do you think this kind of honesty and goodness happens everywhere? Just another reason to love small-town Italy.

From Maiori, we must drive once again along the Amalfi Coast until we reach the entrance to the autostrada. Then it is a straight ride to Rome on the best autostrada in Italy, true to Gaetano's description. He is right, so we arrive at Rome's airport to return the car with no problem. According to the odometer I can now proclaim that I have 1200 miles of driving experience in Italy. For my first time driving here, I am satisfied with my performance; however the decision to drive from Rome to Sicily and back in five days is not very economical. With all the low-cost flights within Italy, I can purchase a round-trip ticket to Sicily for much less than the cost of a rental car, tolls, and diesel fuel. In the future, a better option would be to drive to Colle d'Anchise from Rome, return the car somewhere else on the mainland, and then fly to Sicily and back. Live and learn. To my relief, the process of returning the rental car turns out to be so much easier than the fiasco the first day.

From the airport we take a taxi to the hotel, conveniently located near the Fiumicino airport, and directly across from the beach. After a quick check-in, Sue and I go out for dinner at a nearby recommended seafood restaurant, *Amelinda*. It is packed, so I assume the food must be good. Just inside the door of the restaurant are several large tanks of live fish to select for your dinner. Not to disappoint, I have pasta pomodoro, but Sue chooses seafood.

After dinner we are packing our bags for the last time. Since I have access to Wi-Fi at the hotel, I decide to check our flight status before going to sleep. Imagine my surprise to find that the 11:50AM flight from Rome in the morning is now delayed and rescheduled to leave Rome at 3:00PM. Of course that means I will undoubtedly miss my connection to West Palm from Philadelphia. After recovering briefly from this unexpected shock, I call US Air via Skype and speak to someone about this change.

The customer service agent at US Air informs me that I am already re-booked on an 11:00AM flight to Charlotte, and my arrival into West Palm is earlier than my originally scheduled flight. Sue, however, is still booked on the delayed flight to Philadelphia. After much conversation between the agent and Sue and myself, we ultimately are successful in getting Sue booked on the same outbound flight as mine, allowing her to make her connection to Atlanta from Charlotte. There is nothing like last-minute stress, but at least we know about it before arriving at the airport in the morning, which would be so much worse. Of course now I am wired and can't fall sleep until 1:00AM, and we have to be up early to allow time for security at the airport.

At 6:30AM I am awake, in time to have a quick breakfast, pack the last minute things, check in online for the flight and be ready when the shuttle driver picks us up at 8:15AM. He arrives early and we are at Terminal 5 at Rome's Fiumicino Airport in no time.

Standing outside the doors to the airport are three Italian policemen, one armed with a machine gun ready to fire. Scary. No wonder Italian airports do not require passengers to take off their shoes with this kind of security. Check-in is simple, and the lines are not too long, although my carry-on bag sets off an alarm, requiring a manual check by security personnel. The Italian agents open every single thing inside my bag, including a makeup bag. Apparently there is a pair of manicure scissors inside, but they allow them to go through after examination procedures, saying the scissors are small. Imagine getting through the TSA in the States with scissors? Even at the airport things are different in Italy.

The flight back to the States is an eleven-hour flight to Charlotte and then another hour and a half to West Palm for me, and the same time to Atlanta for Sue. Both of us feel that we are ready to go home

2013

Excitement and Disappointment

I have no thoughts of returning to Italy for a while, maybe in two years, or so I think. But just a few months after being home from my latest Italian adventure, driving 1200 miles in a rented Mercedes, I receive a phone call from my sister-in-law Monica. "Guess what? Your brother Rick is ready to go back to Italy, and he really wants to go to Sicily. We want to know if you'd like to come with us."

"Really? You caught me by surprise. I hadn't planned to go back so soon. Let me think about it, and I will let you know shortly," I say. Immediately memories of beautiful Taormina and cobblestoned streets in Cesarò flood my mind and I already envision myself back in Sicilia.

Within a few hours I know that I want to join Monica and Rick, and I phone Monica. "Yes, I do want to come with you to Italy!" So now I help devise another trip, this time to Sicily, the Amalfi Coast, and a couple of days in Rome. Since Rick is such a fitness nut and cyclist, he is eager to time the trip so he can see part of the *Giro d'Italia*, cycling's second biggest race in the world. The event occurs every May so our travel plans must coincide with a stage of the race. We do not yet know the race route and schedule but at the end of September or beginning of October, an official announcement will be made by the race organizers.

"I'm sure one of the stages will be in Sicily, because last year's race did not include any Sicilian towns. Usually every other year one stage occurs there," Rick says.

"That will be great. I wish we knew now about the schedule," I say.

At the end of September the route of the Giro is announced. Although we are surprised and a little disappointed that none of the stages of the race are scheduled for Sicily, we are thrilled that the route of Stage 3 is scheduled on the Amalfi Coast road. So the travel research for flights and hotels begins, and we book accommodations at Hotel Olimpico, outside of Salerno for three nights because of my excellent experience there last year. Expecting the rooms to fill up fast anywhere along the race, we are happy to secure these rooms, through direct e-mail with Gaetano, the hotel's owner, even before we book our flights.

The three of us talk almost daily by phone as we discuss our itinerary. "Hey, I have a thought: How about if we stay an extra day, so we'll have more time on the Amalfi Coast," I suggest.

"I like it. That way maybe Monica will be able to see Positano since she was sick and missed going with us on the bus in 2007," Rick says.

"I'll e-mail Gaetano and see if the hotel has any more availability for us to extend our stay," I say.

Gaetano is very accommodating. So we now have a fourth night booked at the Olimpico. We are so looking forward to our stay. This trip provides us with ten days in Sicily, four on the Amalfi Coast, and the last two in Rome.

Right after Christmas we book flights on Delta, which allow us to fly all the way to Catania, Sicily, with a stop in Rome. "I am glad we are able to book the flights straight to Catania," says Monica.

"I know," I say. "I think that the bags should be checked through, although I think we may have to go through customs in Rome. I am not totally sure if we have to retrieve bags there or not. I guess we'll find out." *Vediamo*. We'll see.

Now, in March, our trip is about to start in almost four weeks. Monica and I are pretty leery about Rick's condition. My brother cannot walk more than two tenths of a mile without a lot of pain. Still very much affected from a cycling accident five and a half weeks ago, he is not yet healed from a fractured pelvis and fractured collarbone. His level of pain is improving, but now his back is the issue.

At best, Italy is a place where you have to be halfway fit to get around. There is so much walking and the streets are uneven and made of cobblestones in most places. I remember the steps and staircases in most towns. Just to get in and out of trains can be a major job, especially with luggage. "No way can he go to Italy like this and walk all over, the way he likes to do." Monica is worried.

"I agree," I say. "He thinks he will be fine, but we know better, don't we?" Of course we do; we are experienced nurses and we agree that he won't be fine four weeks from now to go to Italy. He has an appointment with his orthopedic surgeon Monday, but after discussing the pros and cons, both Monica and I know that the only option is to postpone the trip.

What irony: The whole idea to go to Italy stems from Rick, so we do not want to go without him, although he suggests that alternative. We decide to reschedule for the fall, if we can get vacation time approved. By then he should be good to go.

Our decision turns out to be the right choice, because the verdict from the doctor is both good news and bad news. Apparently his pelvis is healed, and his back has an inflammation and exacerbation of an old injury that will heal eventually. But the collarbone is not stable and he will likely need to have surgery.

"You remember how he kicked my butt in Italy in 2011 with his insistence on walking everywhere, instead of taking public transportation, simply for the sake of getting a lot of exercise," I say.

Monica laughs and agrees. "It's all about the chocolate. He exercises like a lunatic so he can eat chocolate." Rick really is obsessed with being fit. Too bad this tendency hasn't worn off on me.

My brother, however, does not expect to hear of postponing our trip; he still thinks that he can go to Italy now. "I'm fine. I can go right now," he tells us. I believe it is inherent in men's genes, or else maybe in the testosterone levels, that cause men to harbor a large degree of denial. I observe it all the time at the hospital with male patients.

"What do you think about the fall? I may be able to have vacation time approved then. To get time off in the summer is impossible at this late date. Rick probably won't be ready to go until September anyway, right?" I say.

"I think the fall might work. I should be able to have other nurses cover for me so I can go then too," Monica says. "Why don't you request the time off and we can start researching changes for the travel arrangements?"

"OK. I'll see what I can do and then let you know," I say.

So for now, Rick's job is to get better, and Monica and I switch our focus toward the fall.

Sicily Rescheduled

In anticipation of Rick's complete recuperation from his injuries by September, I submit my formal vacation request at work for that month. I am waiting for it to be approved; only then can we change the flights and hotel reservations. Luck is with us: The hotels we booked already, except one, are refundable. An agent at Booking.com agrees to contact the hotel in Catania. "I think we can get the management to change the reservation to the September dates without your losing the prepaid $1000 for the two rooms for five nights. Of course there is no guarantee, but usually the hotels agree to work with us. I will let you know."

While we wait to hear the outcome on the Catania hotel dates, we cancel our nonrefundable tickets from Delta, and kick ourselves for not purchasing travel insurance. Without it, the penalty to change an international flight is $250 per person. After a week or two of checking things, making phone calls, and securing another vacation at work for

September, we are fortunate. When we explain the situation to the airline, Delta generously waives the penalty for all three of us. We also luck out with the hotel, thanks to the customer service agents at Booking.com. They are able to communicate with the Catania hotel through phone calls and e-mails to allow us to change the dates without losing any money. Today a phone call from *Dehan,* a customer service representative at Booking.com, gives me the good news that both rooms are now rebooked for September.

I am able to change the other reservations myself since they are not prepaid, and our rental car is not yet booked. From this situation I learn two valuable lessons: one is to always buy travel insurance (How can I forget: I know better from previously writing an article about the benefits of buying travel insurance). The second lesson is to never purchase nonrefundable hotel reservations even if they cost less.

So the plans for the trip seem to be going well. We hope that Rick does not require surgery, but if he does, he is prepared to follow medical advice. And four weeks later, I am happy that Rick is making progress. Although he still wears a sling, he manages to get his exercise in, even if it is not on a bicycle. "I'm walking at least eight miles a day, some days more, plus doing five miles on the recumbent bike at the gym," he says.

"That's great, Rick. I know you will be walking plenty in Italy, and it looks like you will be ready." I had better kick it into high gear to keep up with him in September, I remind myself.

By mid-July I am confident that I leave again for *Bella Italia* in less than two months, and yes, I am excited. Rick is finally fully recovered from his injuries. He is back to biking fifty miles at a time and also walking between five and eight miles a day.

Our itinerary has us flying to Catania, the second-largest city in Sicily. We plan to spend ten days in Sicily, traveling to new areas and also visiting with our Savoca family there. One of the more exciting plans we have in place is for Monica and me to take a cooking class. After exhaustive research, we finally decide on a reasonably-priced class at an agriturismo about an hour away from Palermo. I am psyched about this and promise *Filippo,* the owner of *Agriturismo Tarantola,* to call a few days ahead and re-confirm.

We also plan to visit Siracusa and *Agrigento*, two cities that are new to us. Next, our itinerary takes us to Palermo for four nights to explore the city, as well as neighboring towns that sound so appealing.

After Sicily we expect to fly to Naples, then take a train to Salerno, where we have reservations at the wonderful Hotel Olimpico in nearby Pontecagnano. This town is our base for three days as we visit historic Pompeii before we return to Sorrento, as well as the Amalfi Coast.

Lastly, we fly to Rome for our final two days. Naturally we plan to spend time in our favorite neighborhood of *Trastevere*, and have a cappuccino and *brioche* at *Bar Quadrani*. Who knows what else? My intent is to blog from Italy, post photos, and take plenty of notes this trip.

One more week and all is well. My brother is back to normal: walking, working out at the gym, and cycling. "I'm ready to go. I've been ready," Rick assures me. In anticipation of long walking days with him in Italy, my athletic shoes are already packed.

Like Rick, I am ready too; most of my clothes are packed. My goal is to take a medium-size bag weighing no more than thirty-five to forty pounds. Although the limits on Delta for international travel are fifty pounds per bag without paying for extra weight, the restrictions for flights within Italy are more stringent. On our flight from Palermo to Naples, the limit for a checked bag is forty pounds, plus a carryon, which cannot weigh more than ten kilograms, or twenty-two pounds. And I recall that, even at thirty-five pounds, my bag is heavy, particularly when lugging it up the steps onto a train. Just thinking about those experiences motivates me to keep my luggage as light as I can.

Ten days in Sicily seems ideal, so I hope to see different parts of this amazing island. I am curious about Siracusa and Agrigento and look forward to spending a lot more time in Palermo, as well as also visiting some towns on the northwestern coast.

Sicily in September

Today, September 12th, I am leaving for Sicily. I chat with the friendly ticket agents at the Delta desk at Palm Beach International Airport as they process my boarding papers. Since it is midmorning on a weekday, no crowds are here, and both Mark and Rick seem enthusiastic to talk with me about their own travel experiences in Italy. "Okay, your bags are booked all the way through to Catania. Hope you have a great time. I have been to Italy, but not to Sicily," Mark says.

"Thank you," I say. "If you have been to Italy, then you know how beautiful it is. Sicily is where my grandparents came from, and the people there are so friendly. I have even been invited into their homes without knowing them."

"Really? Sicily sounds like a great place. We'll have to go there on one of our next trips, Mark."

"Yes, definitely," Mark says. These two agents admit not knowing much about Sicily but are eager to hear me share stories about my solo travel. As I listen to them tell me about their travel adventures in Europe, I think about the benefits and travel opportunities that airline personnel enjoy. Maybe I should have chosen a different career, I ponder. Oh well, too late now.

Before I leave, I hand them my business cards in the hopes that they might check out my book.

I board the flight to Atlanta without incident or delay. I am fortunate to sit next to another person who has a love of Italy. On occasion I engage a person in conversation on a flight, and Greg seems especially interesting as soon as he starts to talk about Italy. "My wife and I have been to Italy several times, and we just love it. Some of our favorite places are Positano, Assisi, and Taormina."

"I know all those places and enjoy them too. Positano and Taormina are beautiful, with their amazing views to the sea, and Assisi is so peaceful," I say. Before too long the flight attendant welcomes us to Atlanta. I hand Greg a business card and mention my book. Not planning on doing marketing in an airport and on a flight today, I surprise myself. Thank you, Greg, for an enjoyable conversation and the tip about your favorite Italian liqueur, *Amaro del Capo*.

Once inside Atlanta's Hartsfield-Jackson Airport, I make my way to Gate F and have a seat while I wait for my flight to Paris. Due to the need to change the reservations from spring to fall, the direct flight to Italy, unfortunately, now includes a layover in Paris. Any disappointment I feel ends as soon as I catch a glimpse of Rick and Monica walking toward the check-in desk. Thrilled to see them, I smile and stand up to greet them with hugs. "Hi. It's great to see you. How was the flight from Savannah?"

Monica hugs me back and says, "It was good. No problems."

"Rick, you look good, ready for Italy," I say to my brother. He smiles and nods.

"I told you I was ready to go." While we wait until our zone is called to board, we notice the majority of passengers in line for this Air France flight are not Americans. Monica makes a subtle sign to me with her nose accompanied by a facial grimace of disapproval.

"Mmm, huh, very noticeable. Not pleasant," I say. The overpowering smell of body odor cannot be missed and I instantaneously recall that cultural differences regarding body aromas exist between Americans and the French. What some find sexy, others find disgusting. At this point I am glad that the three of us have seats together so I am not sitting next to anyone with this unbearable smell.

The transatlantic flight is uneventful although my sleep consists of only short catnaps. Glad to disembark the plane this morning after the long travel time, I have no idea of the chaos that awaits us at Charles de Gaulle Airport. As we follow the crowd, we make our way to a security checkpoint inside the airport. Here, we must go through examinations similar to those we know from the TSA in the States. After this process we walk to another terminal where we find ourselves in a hall with at least five hundred other passengers. No signs or overhead messages inform us as to what is happening and we have no clue as to whether we are even in the correct line. Apparently this is an immigration checkpoint, which is mandatory, although unexpected by me. I am under the mistaken impression that immigration occurs in Rome but apparently it occurs at the first point of entry into the European Union.

The lines do not appear to be moving, so Rick, Monica, and I are frustrated and tired. "Do you know what is going on?" Rick says.

"No, I don't. This is so disorganized. I am worried we might not make our connecting flight to Rome," I say. "Let me ask someone to explain the delay and let us know what is happening here."

Once I find an English-speaking border patrol agent I ask about the lines, but he does nothing to calm my nerves. "I don't know why it is like this today. The lines are never this long," is his only comment.

Great, I think, seething inside. This idiot works here and knows nothing. My impressions of the French today are quickly going from bad to worse. Eventually more of the immigration windows are opened up and the lines begin to move. After twenty minutes we are finally at the windows where the agents inspect our passports. My stress level is at an all-time high as I am still not at all sure that we will make our connecting flight.

The French policeman behind my immigration window never cracks a smile, never says hello, nor gives any indication of a sense of urgency. Maybe this is part of the persona that goes with his job description, although I notice that other immigration agents do not appear so stern.

At 9:15AM we reach Gate 754 and our flight to Rome is scheduled to leave at 9:45AM, so I expect to board at any time. I cannot wait to leave this airport and be on my way to Italy. As we take note of our surroundings, I become aware of the sign indicating that our flight is delayed and will not depart until 10:10AM. So after all the stress and worry and rush to reach the gate, we now must wait another hour for our plane to leave Paris. I am even more exasperated.

At long last we are on board the two-hour flight to Rome. I am able to sleep during part of the flight, but once I awaken, I am served a snack of *rosemarino taralli*, a crunchy, cracker-like snack flavored with rosemary. As I savor this Italian snack along with a Coca Light, I smile knowing that I am getting closer to Italy.

I may, in fact, be flying over Italy right now. Although I am sitting in an aisle seat, the Air France pilot banks the plane just enough to the right, so that I am able to catch a glimpse out the window of the magnificent snow-covered

Alps. Such natural beauty impresses me as if I were seeing these mountains for the first time.

I smile again as I overhear a conversation in English by another passenger. This older man is speaking with pride about his grandfather from Messina. He is explaining to a younger gentleman the story about his ancestor arriving in America, a familiar tale, which reminds me of my own grandparents. That comfortable feeling of being home returns as I sense that I am in Italian air space and soon will be on the ground in Rome. Today Rome is just a stopping point for two hours until I reach my final destination of Catania this afternoon. Touchdown is at noon at Rome's Fiumicino Airport. I feel energized despite the few hours of interrupted sleep. I know I will sleep well tonight.

Since Rick, Monica, and I are flying Alitalia Airlines from Rome to Catania, we must retrieve boarding passes at the check-in desk. We have no problems obtaining these. This airport apparently operates with more efficiency than the Charles de Gaulle in Paris.

We have some time before the flight, so Rick offers to watch the luggage, while Monica and I wait in line at the bar to order something light to eat and drink, cappuccino, Coca Light, and a brioche. The only seating available is outside the bar, where Rick sits with the luggage. "We can have our drinks here, and then afterward, you can find the Vodafone store. You said you wanted to buy an Italian SIM card, right?" Monica says.

"Yes, I see the shop around the bend," I say.

With my unlocked Blackberry phone I am able to insert an Italian SIM card, which then allows me to make and receive calls and texts within Italy without costing a fortune. For 35€ I buy a card good for 350 minutes, 250 texts, and 1 GB of data. Although I am the only one in the store, the process takes a long time, partly because the system is slow and partly due to the young female employee chit-chatting with a young male employee. Priorities like these are elements of the Italian lifestyle, and I know that well.

Again: nothing happens fast in Italy, so I am not surprised that our 2:00PM flight to Catania is now delayed until 2:30PM. *Molto lento*. Very slow.

As we wait to board the flight, my attention is drawn to the fashions on display by the Italian passengers. Their stylish apparel is in sharp contrast to American travelers who opt for comfort before style. No wonder Italians can spot American tourists by our dress. So now I pretend to have a front row seat at a fashion runway show as I observe a man whose jeans are cut very tight. The pink sneakers are a nice extra touch. A woman, who is probably fifty yet appears very toned and fit, wears an outfit more commonly seen on teen-aged girls. I am glad that I am back in Italy to enjoy conversations in Italian, as well as watching people again.

Once we are allowed to board, the process is not as easy as simply walking onto the plane. Instead, the passengers walk outside to a waiting shuttle bus, which then transports us to a location farther out on the tarmac where our waiting plane is parked and ready to load. I do not mind the walk on this sunny day. The weather here is perfect—warm and sunny, but not too hot.

At 2:45PM I am sitting in the plane, waiting to fly to Catania. I'm tired and can't wait to go to sleep tonight. "We've been up over twenty-four hours," I say to Rick and Monica.

"I know. I'm exhausted. I didn't sleep much at all on the plane," says Rick.

"Me neither," says Monica.

"I know. It's hard to sleep on these planes, although I did manage to sleep a little at a time," I say. The flight to

Catania takes an hour and a half, during which I am able to doze a little more. At 3:50PM the plane touches down, and we make our way to the familiar green and white sign in the Alitalia baggage claim area, *Alitalia ritiro bagagli*. One more time we must proceed through the immigration lines with our luggage, but this experience is much more laid back than at major airports.

I guess I should assume that the airport in Paris, which is Europe's second busiest airport, handling over 61 million passengers a year, might be more chaotic than this smaller *Catania–Fontanarossa Airport*. Although Catania's field is Sicily's busiest, only six million passengers pass through here each year, and that is only one-tenth the number handled by Charles de Gaulle Airport in Paris. Thus we are able to quickly find ground transportation. "Can you take us to the Excelsior Grand Hotel? Do you know it?" I say.

Like most taxi drivers in a tourist city, this man understands English and nods as he repeats back the name of the hotel to me. He sets his GPS for our hotel and we are on our way. The short taxi ride from the Catania airport confirms for me that I am indeed in Italy. It reminds me once again how crazy the drivers can be here. After all the planning and waiting, I am finally in Sicily!

By 5 o'clock we reach the familiar entrance to our four-star hotel. Check-in goes smoothly. I think we may even have the same rooms as last time. The view of Etna is somewhat obscured by clouds, but we still have a view of the volcano from our hotel room windows. Perhaps in the morning I will have a better photo op. After freshening up and unpacking, Rick, Monica, and I head out to walk some and explore the area near the hotel. "I need to find some big bottles of water," Monica says.

"Yes, maybe we can find a supermercato while we are out. I'd like some Coca Light," I say.

We find our desired beverages, and while we are near the hotel, we also look for Al Carpaccio, a restaurant we like here. I still smile when I recall having to ring a bell and wait for the owner to personally welcome us inside. We look forward to returning to his *ristorante* tonight, our first evening in Catania, although we do not see Al Carpaccio anywhere. "I know it is just around the corner from the hotel," I say; yet we don't seem to find it. After walking up and down several streets, we ask a few locals and their responses surprise me. Not one of them is familiar with the restaurant, which seems strange to me. After at least an hour of looking and asking different local residents, we finally discover a closed and locked shop, with the typical dark grey aluminum rolling door covering the front. The place appears deserted and no longer open for business. Sadly, we realize that this is what is left of Al Carpaccio. Disappointed and hungry, the three of us decide to try Monica's suggestion of a small place, *Pasta and Pizza,* on *Via M. Ventimiglia.* We learn that the restaurant is owned by two young brothers who speak some English and even have a Facebook page. I am impressed with their motivation to operate their own business, especially in these hard economic times, when so many young Italians are unemployed. Of course we order pasta pomodoro and insalata mista for our first dinner in Sicily. Our meals taste delicious. Despite the simple name of their establishment, neither the food nor the service disappoints. Soon afterward, I am happy to snuggle down in a comfortable bed; by nine thirty I am asleep.

Our colazione on the outside terrace is relaxing and inviting. Monica and I savor especially the cappuccino. Despite the full spread, we choose fruit, yogurt, and pastry. "Did you notice all those film trucks parked in front of the hotel as you walked through the lobby?" I say.

"Yes," Monica says. "I saw some of the film crew too. One of the actors was changing clothes outside of one of the trucks."

"Really? I bet he didn't think anyone could see him, or else he didn't care. I wonder what they are filming."

After our morning meal we head out for a walk and some exercise. Across the street from the hotel is the courthouse where the real action happens. Interesting. Live filming is taking place while a small crowd is watching. We learn that the movie, *Stella Maris*, is directed by *Giacomo Abbruzzese*, and that this particular setting is commonly used for films made in Sicily.

We make a few stops to purchase some items we need. Then Rick and I go to the rental car office to pick up the car, but he does not think to bring his passport. "No passport, no car," the young female Italian agent informs him. She is able, though, to call our hotel, knowing that they keep a record of guests' passports, so all is good. We drive the Alpha Romeo Giulietta back to the hotel, park it in the underground garage, and then meet up with Monica for another walk down Corso Italia. We end up at the busy Caffè Europa to refresh ourselves.

Glad that I have my unlocked Blackberry with an Italian SIM card, I phone Teresa and Angela to make arrangements to meet them. We invite Angela for dinner tonight and confirm our visit with Teresa tomorrow in Cesarò. Since it is early afternoon, we decide to drive to Taormina and to *Castelmola*, the hill town above Taormina.

We are more than familiar with Taormina and, as usual, the streets are crowded. My agenda here in Taormina is to find a particular jewelry shop that my daughter-in-law likes. "I am going to walk down this street to the address of the jewelry store. It shouldn't take long. Do you want to wait here in the piazza for me?" I ask Monica and Rick.

"Sure, no problem," Monica says. "We'll be here."

"Okay, I'll see you soon," I say, as I walk toward the address 174 on *Corso Umberto*. I find the address within five minutes, but the name of the shop is not what I expect. A similar shop exists in this spot and the employee informs me that the store I seek is no longer here. This situation occurs frequently in Italia, and probably even more often with the current deplorable economic climate. So, when I visit Rome later this trip, I will try to find the shop of the same name; supposedly one exists there.

Next we drive to Castelmola but discover that we are actually still in Taormina. So we opt to take a bus the remaining six kilometers up to the hilltop village.

The bus tickets are well worth the cost of just under three euros each to take the twenty-minute ride up the hill to Castelmola. The road has more S-bends than I expect and at times the bus is forced to stop and wait for the oncoming vehicles to back down the hill. A good choice not to drive this road ourselves. The bus driver is quite skilled in navigating the narrow, winding roads, His reactions to other drivers provide us with entertainment.

Not having to drive to Castelmola and having to carefully watch the foot traffic, as well as the rules of the road, the three of us can enjoy the stunning surrounding countryside. Because the elevation is so much higher, we can see green hills interspersed with tall Italian cypress trees. The view all the way down to the Ionian Sea is worth the dizzying ride.

In the same piazza where the bus stops, I quickly locate the famous Bar Giorgio, an establishment here since 1907 and famous for *Vino alle Mandorle*, an almond dessert wine. I buy two bottles of that wine plus some *Torrone* candy to take home. I am content and rejoin Rick and

~ 173 ~

Monica, who are taking in the views from the piazza before we return to Taormina on the same bus, which is still parked in the piazza.

In Taormina we retrieve our car and drive to meet our friend, Angela, for dinner at La Bussola, our favorite restaurant in Giardini-Naxos. Angela is waiting for us since we are fifteen minutes late. She looks so pretty in heels and a black-and-white dress with a matching jeweled belt. For the first time, she is not wearing a scarf. "*Ciao*, Angela, it's so good to see you. No scarf this time?"

After she gives me a hug, she shakes her head and says, "No, it is too hot. *Fa tempo caldo*." She is right; the temperatures in Catania and Taormina range in the 80s since our arrival. Rick and Monica take turns hugging Angela. "Let's head to the restaurant," I say.

We choose to sit outside, and the waiter promptly provides us with menus and explanations of the specials of the day. Of course Angela orders a seafood platter, and the three of us each order something different, but not fish. Rick chooses *vitello cotoletta,* veal cutlet, and I try the special, *casarecce alla norma* with vitello cotoletta. Casarecce, we learn, means homemade, so even the pasta we order is made from scratch. Casarecce alla norma is a typical Sicilian dish made with tomatoes, fried eggplant, grated ricotta cheese, and basil. Monica orders the casarecce pomodoro.

We do enjoy our meals, which include a wonderful dessert of *semifreddo* and a lemon sorbet. This is my first time trying semifreddo, which means semi-frozen. "Angela, what is semifreddo basically?" I say.

"It tastes really good. You should try it. It is a little like ice cream but not really. It is softer." Mmmm. She is right. This delicious dessert is served with a presentation that makes it almost too good to eat. The white custard-looking serving is covered with sliced almonds, adorned with strawberry slices, and drizzled with chocolate sauce.

We enjoy having Angela to ourselves tonight. Her English is so good now that Rick and Monica appreciate the conversation with her more than at their earlier visit.

After our delectable meal, we set up a tentative agenda with Angela about the next few days with her family. Tomorrow the plan is to go to Cesarò, where we will meet up with Teresa and visit her parents. "Too bad you have to work tomorrow, Angela. I wish you could come with us to Cesarò," I say.

"I know. Me too. I asked for these days off and they scheduled me to work," Angela says. "But I will see you Monday when we will go to Caltagirone."

"Yes, we'll have a good time again," I say.

When we casually walk back to our cars, Angela is only ten minutes from her home, and we say buonanotte.

As I listen to the soft waves roll against the rocks near the shore, and feel the warm night breeze against my face, I feel so at home! For me there is nothing that compares to being near the water. Where I live we call it the ocean; in Sicily they call it the sea; it is one and the same. *Bellissimo!*

Family Time in Sicily

I am looking forward to the visit with our dear friends, the Savoca family, today. In a happy mood I enter the terrace of the Excelsior Grand Hotel, where its staff serves breakfast, and where Rick and Monica are already seated at a small table.

"*Buongiorno, ciao*," Monica says. "Did you see that farmers market set up outside our hotel, Margie?" Monica says.

"Yes, I saw it from my window. Do you want to check it out after breakfast?"

"Sure, maybe we can find a plant to take to Maria in Cesarò today."

"That's a great idea, Monica. And maybe, if they have some Sicilian cookies, we can take those too."

At the market we select a potted plant. The farmer who

sells us the cookies explains with pride that they are made from the wheat on his farm outside of Sigonella.

At the supermercato we pick up some Coca Light and some detergent to wash clothes later. "Let's drop these items off at our rooms and be on our way to Cesarò," I say.

The weekend traffic in Catania slows driving down to a crawl. "It takes forever to get through this city," Rick says. "Driving here is just crazy."

Once outside the city limits, we appreciate the less chaotic drive through the scenic campagna. We notice cactus bearing fruit of prickly pears, as well as Mt. Etna looming high above us to the north. No train routes exist here on the way to Cesarò, and I can feel the gradual increase in elevation as we drive farther along SA 284. Every once in a while a house is interspersed among the trees, and I like the contrast to the hectic city pace.

We all notice how the edge of the road is strewn with trash. Such a shame in a place with so much natural beauty. "It must be that these towns don't have the funds to pay someone to keep it clean," Monica says.

"But who throws out all the trash in the first place?" I wonder. "Don't the local residents take pride in keeping their countryside clean, or is this trash thrown here by travelers?" One of the not-so-nice aspects to life in Sicily.

Along the road we pass vendors selling prickly pears and other fruit, and we pass cyclists out for a morning ride to Bronte.

After apparently taking a wrong turn, we end up driving through the town of Bronte. This town is full of narrow, swerving streets, a lot like Cesarò. We recognize the cyclists we overtook, and who are gathered here after their ride. Bronte looks interesting, and I would like to explore the town in the future. Today, however, we are expected in Cesarò around noon, since we are invited for lunch at the home of Teresa's parents.

Before we reach our destination, we stop at Bar Central, the first place open, so we can use the restroom. Not a pleasant place, because there is no toilet paper.

I recall Teresa warning us about the lack of accuracy of the GPS in these small villages. "*No navigazione,*" is her advice and she is right, because we are not able to locate the house on *Via Piano Ramusa* easily. But we arrive there at twelve-thirty.

Maria is standing on the balcony and smiles as soon as she sees us. "*Ciao, Maria,*" I say. *Siamo felici di vederti.*

Come stai? Hi, Maria. We are happy to see you. How are you?

"Ciao, ciao," Maria says, as she disappears inside.

Teresa meets us at the front door and ushers us inside the two-story home. "*Ciao,* Margie. *Ciao,* Monica and Rick. Welcome." Teresa is always so kind, and is eager to speak some English mixed with her native language. "Please come inside."

"*Grazie,* Teresa. So good to see you again." Hugs and kisses of course complete the reception before we walk up the steps to see her parents.

"Something smells good in here," says Monica.

"*Sì,* I am cooking," says Teresa as she nods toward the kitchen. Since her parents are in their late seventies and early eighties, Teresa helps out whenever she can.

"*Siamo così felici di essere qui,* I say. "*Grazie per averci invitato a pranzo.*" We are so happy to be here. Thank you for inviting us for lunch.

Maria Teresa's father, Antonino, is happy to see us and offers us seats at the kitchen table, which is already set with plates and utensils. "*Buongiorno, signore. Grazie,*" Rick says as he sits down.

"*Ecco alcuni biscotti per voi, signora,*" says Monica. Here are some cookies for you, signora.

When we present Maria with the plant and the cookies she is obviously thrilled and her smile becomes even bigger. "*Grazie,*" she says as she opens the bag and samples one of the cookies immediately. I guess she has a sweet tooth like me. Monica and I don't miss this subtle action, and we smile. With Teresa here to help translate, because her parents speak only Sicilian, the conversation goes smoothly. Lunch is fantastic; the rigatoni pomodoro is served with homemade sauce. The ample meal includes sausage, figs, mulberries, grapes, homemade red wine, and tasty Sicilian bread from the *panificio*, the bakery, in Taormina.

This delicious meal in their home is one hundred times better than the terrible pizza from *Bar Saraniti* two years ago. After lunch we offer to take Antonino out to the countryside, his favorite place, so he can show us his property and the country house where he likes to spend time. Teresa tries to warn us about the rough terrain and suggests we take two cars. Antonino is obviously happy to be going to his other home ten minutes away.

When we arrive, he shows us around the inside of the simple three-room home, and then leads a tour outside. Here he points out his almond and olive trees, as well as a persimmon tree, and more. I can tell that this man is proud of what he considers his country getaway. He takes time to show Rick the self-made fences and cistern. Sitting on a chair outside the house, Maria wants to chew on a piece of chicory, so Teresa picks a few for her from the ground, where it appears to be growing wild. The scene here is one of tranquility and quiet. *Il dolce far niente.*

After almost an hour in this peaceful retreat we say goodbye so we can spend a little time in the town and on *Via Monte Pieta*, the one-time address of our grandfather's home. We are disappointed when we reach this dwelling, though, and discover that now a padlock is on the door. "What is this? I don't remember this lock being here before," Rick says.

"It wasn't there before. It doesn't look like anyone lives here anymore," Monica says.

"But last time we came, remember the woman who came out from the house next door and told us that her cousin lived here?" I say.

Some men are operating heavy machinery just around the corner, and we ask them if they know about this house. "*In quella casa non ci abita nessuno. E` vuota da molti anni.*" No one lives there. The house has been vacant for many years.

"That doesn't make any sense," I say to my brother and sister-in-law. "Just two years ago the neighbor told us her cousin lived in that house." Rick wanders around the corner and Monica and I follow. The house on the corner, which seems to be adjacent to my grandfather's home, is partially gutted; that is what these workers are doing. We can see inside as an entire exterior wall is down. "I think this wall is on the other side of Grandpa's house," Rick says.

"Too bad we can't go inside. I was really looking forward to this, but now it looks like it isn't ever going to happen."

"That's a shame," Monica says. "We might as well leave." With no option of meeting an owner and possibly entering the house, Rick and Monica turn and walk back down the street. My hopes for a look inside are dashed, and I feel sad. I think if I were here alone, I might wander around some more, or even wait to see if a neighbor might appear, which is probably denial on my part. Slowly, I follow my brother and sister-in-law, but turn back for one last look at Grandpa's house.

I still feel this strong connection to my ancestry as I walk down that sloped street; I daydream about what my grandfather's life must have been like in the late nineteenth and early twentieth centuries. A sobering thought.

I guess I still suffer some effect of jet lag; it's 3:30 in the morning and I am still wide awake despite an eventful day. Or is it not my body that keeps me awake but my emotions? I hope I can fall asleep soon.

Now at nine thirty I am rested and ready to meet Monica and Rick for breakfast. As I look out the window I notice the streets are wet from an early morning rain, but the weather seems to be improving.

"This is a great breakfast. I can't believe the selection," I say to Monica.

"I know, they have several types of yogurt. Did you see the sweet rolls?"

"Oh yes, almost a table full of them, including cakes. I am fine with yogurt and granola mixed in, a little fruit, and of course, cappuccino," I say.

"As long as they have fruit, I am fine," Rick says, always the healthy eater at meals.

"I'm anxious to walk to the farmers market today. This one in Catania is said to be one of the largest in Sicily, from what I have read," I say.

"We can do that," Rick says. "At least it isn't raining. It should be a good day to walk around." After we finish our meal the three of us head out on foot for today's Sicilian adventure.

While we are still walking in *Piazza Giovanni Vergona*, and before reaching Corso Italia, some not-so-pleasant smells of body fluids and animal waste fill the air. "Disgusting, watch where you're stepping. I just passed some dog poop," Monica says.

"I guess it is part of city life, the not-so-good part," I say. In Sicily, and also in mainland Italy, you have to be willing to accept the bad with the good to enjoy the experience.

The colorful outdoor, fresh market lives up to its reputation for being large. The produce looks crisp and clean, and the prices are low. The market area seems to take up several city blocks, and the vendors offer almost any articles you might want. I cannot believe the selection:

fresh cheeses, as well as fresh fish of all types; large and small nuts, plus bundles of fresh herbs. Even a butcher shop is set up outside. Farther down, vendors who are obviously not Italian sell non-food items, including CDs, underwear, shoes, jewelry, purses, and also cell phone cases. One man who catches my eye sells cigarettes for three euros a pack. Marlboro.

Monica and I are looking for cut flowers, and when we do not find any, we ask one vendor who is selling cheese if he knows where flowers might be. *"Scusi, dove sono i fiori?"* Excuse me, where are the flowers? He answers, half in Italian and half in English, *"No fiori.* Would you like some cheese?" I thank him and walk away smiling, as I realize how silly it is for me to think he knows, or is interested in telling me, about flowers. He looks toward his coworkers and laughs, probably thinking, Stupid Americans. They ask a cheese vendor for flowers.

Once we leave the market, Monica and I decide to try an *arancini*. Catania is known for these fried rice balls filled with a variety of other foods, such as cheese, meat, olives, and pomodoro sauce. We buy one at a place called *Panificio Pizze* and share it. Rick is not interested in trying it, but Mo and I like it. The one arancini is more than the two of us can eat; it is very filling.

Inside this same shop Monica notices something for the first time. "Look at this, Margie," Monica says, "pizza with French fries on top."

"You're kidding." I have to see for myself, and she is right. The shop sells individual slices of pizza covered with French fries. This treat is a favorite with children.

We are meeting our friend Angela at the hotel at a quarter to twelve. She is driving an hour from her home in Taormina. The plan is for her to join the three of us as Rick drives us to Caltagirone, where we are invited to lunch at the home of her brother Calogero. His wife, Monica, is one of the best cooks I know, so we expect another amazing food experience.

Angela arrives at the hotel a little early, and Rick directs her to the parking garage so she can leave her car in the underground safe-parking area. Soon after, we leave for Caltagirone in our rented Alfa Romeo with Rick driving.

The traffic through Catania is horrible as usual; it takes nearly a half hour just to get out of the city. "Morons," Rick says of the other drivers. "I can't believe they let these people get on the road." We arrive in Caltagirone after an hour and a half, at two thirty, where Angela's sister-in-law Monica, and Angela's *nipoti*, niece and nephew, Martina and Antonio, greet us. Monica's parents, *Antoinetta* and *Martino*, are visiting from Puglia, as well as another couple, *Maria* and *Lorenzo*; so there is a houseful of people. Calogero is not yet home from his job at the police station but is expected soon. Our arrival is a regular love fest with all the introductions and hugs and kisses. We also are excited to meet the newest member of the Savoca family, baby *Gioia*, who is not even two months old, and adorable. Martina is beaming as the proud mamma and *Adriano*, the baby's pappa, is here too. Despite the fact that no one speaks fluent English besides us and Angela, we have no problem communicating. I am able to practice my Italian and Angela helps out with whatever isn't clear.

The kitchen is a whirlwind of activity with Monica and her mother, Antoinetta, who loves to cook as much as Monica. Both are in various stages of preparation of food and seem happy in their roles.

Calogero is now home, and by three o' clock we are sitting down to lunch in the downstairs kitchen. For the next four hours we are treated to an array of homemade Italian food.

To say that everything tastes so good is definitely an understatement. Maria and Monica serve two types of bruschetta; one is made with bread that Antoinetta brings from her kitchen in Puglia, and the other with bread made by her friend, Maria. We are treated to *funghi*, mushrooms, in olive oil, as well as pepperoncini, which are very hot. The mushrooms are courtesy of Calogero and Antonio's recent forest excursion. As if one type were not enough, Monica also prepares funghi with pomodoro sauce. "*Delicioso*, Monica," I say. She is pleased.

Of course a large bottle of red wine graces the table. I am told that the wine is homemade by either Martino or Lorenzo, one of the two men visiting from Puglia. Fresh *pecorino* cheese from Caltagirone is yet another appetizer. *Pecorino siciliano* is a firm cheese made from sheep's milk. The aging process can be anywhere from three to eighteen months. Percorino is also produced in Rome, *pecorino romano*, Tuscany, *pecorino toscana*, and Sardinia, *pecorino sardo*. While all of these might be imported to the States, I am only familiar with pecorino romano.

We have pasta pomodoro and pasta norma, which is pasta with eggplant, *basilico*, basil, as well as freshly grated Ricotta cheese, from a cousin's farm in Cesarò. I love the pasta norma, especially with the cheese. For the *secondi piatti*, which I must decline since this is just too much food, Monica serves chicken cotoletta, breaded chicken cutlets, and also agnello, lamb. Throughout the meal we do a lot of laughing and everyone seems happy to be together. I notice that all the men sit at one end of the table, and the women sit at the other end. Adriano is the exception, and he sits next to Martina. I feel like I am at home, once again, with my Italian Savoca family, despite our different seating arrangements in the States.

For dessert, we have watermelon. "Melon from America," says Lorenzo, proud to say something in English. We also have *meloni bianchi*, which looks and tastes like cantaloupe, except the texture is not as dense, and the color is white. A fruit bowl overflowing with grapes, plums, and peaches is on the table too. Biscotti are accompanied by espresso with *crema di zucchero*. After all these delicacies, Monica starts frying up zucchini flowers after dipping them in a very light flour mixture. This is my first taste of those, and they are now on the top of my list; I want to try to make them myself. They are crispy and so good, such a tasty, crunchy treat. Monica, as if to make a point, suddenly opens her pantry, to show us a huge orange zucchini.

What a great day with our Savoca family here. I would love it if one day they came to visit us in the States.

At seven fifteen we say arrivederci and leave for the hotel in Catania. On the ride home we all feel the exuberance from the family time together. "Calogero really enjoyed that Skype call with Mom and Dad on your iPad, Monica," Rick says. "He asked me a lot of questions about it and was interested in the technology."

"I know. I think he'd like to have one. Did you see Antonio has an iPod? So their family is pretty hi-tech," Monica says.

"Yes, he was very interested when I showed him how to make a Face Time call at no charge."

"Angela, your new baby niece is adorable. I am so glad we got to meet her. And Adriano seems very caring as a new, young father," I say.

"Yes, Gioia is beautiful. And Martina is a good mother. Adriano is very attentive."

"What a special day this has been, Angela. I am so glad that you were off work today so we could go together to visit your brother and his family," Monica says.

"*Si*, I am too. But now I am tired," Angela says.

"I think we're all tired. And I know that I am not going to be up too late tonight," I say.

We arrive at the hotel at eight thirty. "Goodbye, Angela. Today was a wonderful day with you."

"*Ciao*, good night. I hope to see you again soon, maybe in America." Angela says as she hugs each of us before she drives home to Taormina. Exhausted, we retire to our rooms and go to bed.

Siracusa and Agrigento

While deciding on my choice of breakfast food this morning, I have the good fortune to meet a charming British couple who are traveling in Sicily for ten days. I welcome the opportunity to speak English with other travelers, and I particularly enjoy the British accent. What I believe is so interesting is to hear their perspectives on travel in Italy; I always learn something, even if the conversation is brief, as this one is.

By ten thirty Rick, Monica, and I are heading to the ancient city of Siracusa. By now we are used to the chaos driving out of Catania causes. With Rick as our expert driver we arrive in Siracusa at eleven fifteen.

Since this is my first visit to this city, two landmarks I am especially eager to see are the Greek ruins of the Temple of Apollo and the Greek amphitheatre. My guide book suggests that we park in the *Talete* parking garage at the end of *Via Trieste*. We deposit some coins in the meter and print out our ticket. From here a short walk leads us to *Ortigia* Island, the historic center of Siracusa with its origins from ancient Greece. I am grateful for the information from one of my Twitter friends, Alfredo Vinci. Ortigia is his birthplace and he suggests that this section of Siracusa is a must-see.

As soon as we cross the bridge onto the island, we encounter the ruins of the Temple of Apollo. I am always amazed to see structures that date back so far in time. According to my reading, this landmark is considered the oldest existing Doric temple in Western Europe. Rick points out the sign, *Tempio di Apollo Secolo VI a.C.*, erected in the sixth century BC. A truly incredible sight! As in Rome and other cities in Italy, when I see ancient structures in the middle of a city they seem almost surreal to me.

I love wandering around the narrow alleys of Ortigia, noticing how old most of the buildings are, and wondering about the lifestyle that exists here today. At one point I see a woman on a third-story balcony slowly lowering a basket from one end of a rope. When the basket reaches the street level, a vendor is waiting; he then deposits an item into her basket, and the woman raises it back up to retrieve whatever she buys. The rope can be lowered either from a window or a balcony. This Sicilian tradition is known in Italian as *accettare dalla finestra*, or to accept from the window. But Alfredo explains that "those vendors barely speak Italian," and in Sicilian, "*accattari* is the verb to buy and the basket is called a *panaro.*" The verb *calare*, to lower, is also used and the vendor would say "*calassi u panaru, signora.*" Alfredo recalls calling to his Sicilian *nonna,* grandmother, in a more casual way, "*Nonna, cala u panaru.*"

Grazie, Alfredo, for this language lesson.

I almost feel like stepping back in time here. I like this practical use of such a simple idea. As I wander these crooked streets, I notice many homes and buildings that seem to be in disrepair, and I assume that the money is just not available to correct the problems.

Along the way we meet some American tourists who are leaving Siracusa; they generously offer to give us their map, which we appreciate since we do not have one. "Thanks," says Rick, "this is a big help. We are trying to find Piazza del Duomo."

"We just came from there. Keep walking down here and you will run into it," says the helpful traveler.

"He was a nice guy. We can use the map," I say.

"Okay, let's see where we are," Rick says. In no time he locates our position on the Siracusa map. "We need to walk this way, and then turn left."

On the way to the Duomo, we realize that we are in *Piazza Minerva*, where several restaurants are open for *pranzo*, lunch. One looks particularly interesting, mainly because it seems so modern and has a Greek name, *Kaos*. We are hungry, so we decide to try it. Kaos more than satisfies us with a delicious pizza margherita and insalata mista.

A block away is Piazza del Duomo, which I understand not only from Alfredo, but also from some of my research, to be one of the most beautiful baroque piazzas in Sicily. I am impressed by how white the buildings are, and how clean the piazza is.

Not the typical square piazza, this one is more rectangular. Several impressive buildings front on it, including the remarkable *Palazzo Beneventano del Bosco* with its enclosed courtyard, as well as the *Palazzo del Senato*, which nowadays functions as the Town Hall. At one end of the piazza stands the Church of Santa Lucia. A musician plays an accordion outside the church doors.

The dominating feature of this attractive piazza is of course the cathedral with its magnificent façade. Previously the ancient temple of Athena, the Siracusa Cathedral, or Duomo, still features the original Doric columns. These columns support the cathedral inside as well as outside.

Since the Duomo is open and the entrance fee is only two euros, we decide to go inside, and I am so glad we do. Now we can see how the building that stands here today is the result of enclosing the spaces between the Doric Greek columns of the original temple. Remarkable. Although the interior is not what I would consider elegant, it is indeed amazing by virtue of the existence of its ancient original structures.

I am reminded of other ancient sites on the mainland that are worth the price of admission: the *Pozzo di San Patrizio*, St. Patrick's Well in Orvieto, and *Giotto's* Bell Tower in Florence.

As we prepare to leave the island of Ortigia, we walk along the water's edge and experience memorable views of the crystal water of the Ionian Sea. A shaded park and the marina, which is home to some immense yachts, also capture my interest as I shoot more photos in this paradise.

Just before we cross the bridge to retrieve our car from the garage, I feel the need for a gelato. "Rick and Monica, do you mind if we stop for a gelato? Maybe you want one too, or perhaps a cool drink. It's hot here," I say.

"I don't want a gelato, but I'll have some water," Rick says.

So we backtrack a few feet and stop in at *Bar Apollo*, across from the Temple of Apollo, on Alfredo's recommendation. " *C'e' Paolo?* " I ask one of the waiters for Alfredo's friend, *Paolo*.

A friendly gentleman with a warm smile appears and introduces himself. "*Buon giorno. Sono Paolo.*"

"*Buon giorno, Paolo. Sono Americana e sono amico di Alfredo Vinci*," I say. Hi, Paolo. I am American and a friend of Alfredo Vinci. In Italian, Paolo explains that his friendship with Alfredo goes back to his childhood, and that they are like brothers. This smiling Sicilian man cannot be any nicer, recommending pistachio and *nocciola*, hazelnut gelato, which of course sounds good to me.

He asks Rick and Monica what they would like to have, and Monica says, "*Acqua, non frizzante, per favore. Due.*" Water, without fizz, please. Two.

To sit outside at Bar Apollo on this warm September afternoon is one of the little treats of being in Sicily. I enjoy the ambience and look around, as we take a much-needed break from the heat. Paolo refuses to allow us to pay for anything and then gladly poses for a photo at my request. *Grazie,* from the bottom of my heart, Paolo and Alfredo.

The good feeling of the day suddenly ends when we return to the parking garage to find that our rental car is damaged. An obvious dent and some deep black scratches clearly are present on the right front fender as we approach the Alfa Romeo. "This is just great," Rick says in anger. "Someone hit us and did all this damage. These dents and scratches were not here before."

Naturally, the three of us are upset and take turns inspecting the damage. "There are scratches on the wheel too," Monica says. "With all the crazy driving in Catania and our Alpha Romeo gets damaged in a parking garage, the one place where I would expect it to be safe."

I am aggravated too. "How can someone do damage to another vehicle and take no responsibility? No note is here from someone claiming accountability."

"They must have been parked next to us and hit us as they pulled out of their spot," Rick says. Even though we have insurance on the car, since that is mandatory in Italy, we could be responsible for the deductible of up to €1000. That is roughly $1,300. The feeling of lack of control in this situation hits all of us. Our moods vacillate between anger and disgust.

Since there is nothing we can do to change the unpleasant situation about our car, we now move on to another section of Siracusa, where the Greek amphitheatre is located. Too far to walk, we drive there, park, and pay the entrance fee to this UNESCO World Heritage site, an ancient marvel from Greek times. The original structure dates back to the fifth century BC, with reconstruction two centuries later. Built right into the rock, what remains of the amphitheatre is quite impressive, as many of the original fifty-nine rows of seats are still present. I recall reading that the theatre could hold 15,000 spectators at one time.

Although this amphitheatre is an amazing monument and one of the main attractions of Siracusa, all of us feel a little disheartened after the unfortunate incident with the car. We try to enjoy the time here, and climb the rows of seats to photograph the amphitheatre from various angles, but none of us are too talkative. After an hour walking the grounds here, we drive back to Catania, and arrive at our hotel by six o' clock. On the positive recommendation from the front desk manager, we decide to have dinner at *Pagano Restaurant*, situated behind the hotel. "They serve authentic Sicilian food," she says.

After a meal of rigatoni pomodoro and caprese salad I can now attest to the hotel's favorable review of Pagano.

Tired after a long day, the three of us make a few Skype calls home and then sink into our comfortable beds for a much-needed rest.

The alarm on my phone wakes me at seven thirty this morning, so that I can have time to finish packing and have breakfast before checking out of the hotel and leaving for Agrigento. By ten Rick, Monica, and I are on the road, driving past the port of Catania, where I see a lot of cargo containers stacked up. Near the edge of the city we pass some fruit vendors who are selling meloni bianchi at roadside stands for anywhere from one euro fifty cents to three euros.

We share the road with other cars, buses, trucks, and of course Vespas. The annoying voice on the GPS adds to the frustration of getting out of Catania's crazy traffic for the final time. Within twenty minutes we are on the A-19 autostrada on the way toward Agrigento. The rolling hills with rows of citrus trees along the campagna make for a more soothing scene. Mt. Etna appears huge although the clouds obscure its peak once again. Italian cypress trees and farms dot the landscape, and the farther we drive away from the coast, the fewer palm trees and cactuses we see. Windmills to the south and solar panels to the north are part of the view this morning as we drive along.

I like the countryside of Sicily. I feel relaxed here and enjoy the quiet. I am surprised though, to see an outlet center emerge in the middle of nowhere. Its name is *Siciliani Outlets* and the Gucci store seems so out of place here. As we pass this commercial area, the landscape becomes very rural again. I notice men laboring in fields with no machinery visible during our approach to a small town named *Sacchitello*, high on a hillside. Life here does not seem easy for the native Sicilians.

Although not many trains run throughout Sicily, I see a track near *Caltanissetta*. A diesel station is within view, so we stop to buy gas and pay €1.82/liter for full service. The total price to fill up our car with diesel is €72. Rick checks the damaged right front fender again without saying anything. After driving through some *gallerie*, tunnels, and mountainous terrain, we turn at the Agrigento/Caltanissetta exit at a quarter to twelve.

Driving in this southern part of Sicily is new to me, so I am curious about what I see. As a passenger in the back seat I have the luxury to take in the scenery. Closer to Agrigento, we pass some industrial businesses and several apartments, then a number of ceramics as well as plastics businesses. From the descending road I can see the ocean and again the cactus plants with fruit; olive trees and vineyards appear once more.

We pass yet another commercial center with stores such as H&M and Euronics. Although these may not be household names in the United States, they are large companies in Italy and other parts of the world. H&M is a Swedish clothing company with 3,100 stores in 53 countries. Euronics is Europe's second-largest consumer retailer.

An hour after leaving the autostrada we arrive in Agrigento. Since we cannot check into our hotel until three, we walk across the street and have lunch at *Trattoria dei Templi*, recommended by the front desk clerk. I try their specialty, *cavatelle alla Valle dei Templi*, cavatelli of the Valley of the Temples. Delicious. Cavatelli are small curved pasta pieces with a long rolled edge. This entrée includes pomodoro sauce, eggplant, and cheese.

After lunch we wander around the beautiful grounds of our hotel before we check in. The Valley of the Temples is not far from the hotel; we have a view of one of the temples from the hotel grounds.

By three thirty we complete the check-in process and prepare to visit the Valley of the Temples, one of Sicily's most famous historical, archaeological parks. Rick wants to walk there from the hotel, but Monica and I convince him to drive instead, since we know that visiting this UNESCO World Heritage site will entail a lot of walking. Ticket booths are present at each end of the park and the entrance cost is a very reasonable ten euros. Once there, we leisurely wander around this ancient place in amazement. I cannot get over the fact that these temples with their classic Greek Doric columns are still standing after so many centuries. The remains of seven temples are here; the most preserved date back to the seventh century BC. The Temple of Concord ranks equally with the Greek temple of *Hephaestos* in Athens, considered to be the world's best-preserved Greek temple.

History is not one of my strong points; my memories

from fifth-grade class consist mainly of stomach aches and boredom. I think my ability to learn and my interest in the subject matter is much higher now because these facts and places take on a visual character for me. I am impressed and eager to learn more when I see these preserved monuments from so long ago.

The distance from one end of the park to the other is two and a half kilometers, which is an easy walk. I am glad that we have the time to see each temple and take photographs from different perspectives. Most of the monuments are barricaded with fencing for protection from damage. Some of the temples are more preserved than others, yet the entire site is impressive.

From this hilltop position we see the entire city of Agrigento below. I feel as though I were in ancient Greece as I walk among these intact ruins from so long ago. "I wonder where the people lived and what their lives were like then," I say to my brother and sister-in-law.

"Look over here, Margie. I think this might be where their homes were," Rick says. We can see remnants of stone foundations of homes and try to speculate about ancient life. "This must have been their water supply," Rick says. All of us are fascinated with the arrangements of stones which represent certain aspects of people's lives from past civilizations. I know I am much more interested in history after I visit places as magnificent as the Valley of the Temples.

On the way to the car, we take a different road back on foot although a bus is available. Monica and I both know that walking is the only option, since we are traveling with the exercise-loving Rick. Along the way, we meet some other tourists who are just beginning the trek to the Temple area. Rick seems happy to give them some tips and encouragement. I am glad we are going back to the hotel since it is quite hot now, and the walk is uphill. I am definitely feeling the fact that I am not in shape as I lag behind Monica and Rick.

When we arrive at a fork in the road, I feel fatigued and decide to walk to the hotel, rather than go with my brother and sister-in-law to where the car is parked. However, I mistakenly assume this road is a shortcut. I do not anticipate that I get lost, walk much farther, and have to ask for directions in Italian from three different people before I make it back to the hotel. Unfortunately my phone with the handy Google Maps app is in the hotel room. When I finally arrive back, exhausted and thirsty, Rick and Mo are already in the hotel lobby, waiting for me with looks of concern on their faces. "What happened? We were worried about you," Monica says.

"Thanks," I say, still huffing and puffing from the walk uphill to the hotel. "I guess my sense of direction is not as good as I think. I thought I was close to the hotel when I left you, but I was wrong. I have been walking for over an hour."

Anxious to get cleaned up, I walk upstairs to my room on the second floor and throw myself on the bed. "You idiot," I say to myself. "You ended up walking three times farther than if you had just gone with them." Fifteen minutes later I feel somewhat refreshed and have a sense of composure so I can join Rick and Mo for dinner. We walk down the street to the same place recommended earlier for lunch. Deciding to try some Sicilian seafood, since I am near the coast, I order calamari, but I am disappointed. This is not nearly as good as in other parts of Sicily. The *Nero D'Avola* local red wine helps, though, and I enjoy the caprese salad.

We walk back to the hotel and say goodnight to each other. We need to leave in the morning for Palermo, with a stop in the countryside at an agriturismo for a real Sicilian cooking class.

Driving in Sicily –

More Tales of Getting Lost

"I'm thinking of taking a cooking class in Italy," I tell my sister-in-law on the phone during our planning stages. "I know Rick wouldn't be interested, but he can go for a long walk and get his exercise in while we are at the class. What do you think?"

Monica likes the idea. "Neat, that sounds like fun," she says. "I'll talk with Rick. I am sure he won't care and he can always find something else to do."

During my research for cooking classes in Italy I find varying price levels, ranging from €60 in Rome to €200 in Ravello on the Amalfi Coast. Translated into dollar figures at the euro conversion rate while we are in Italy, the cost is roughly between $78 and $260 per person for a four-hour cooking class, including lunch.

Since I am not a foodie, I certainly do not intend to pay more than $100 for a culinary class, even in Italy. So after shopping around on the internet, I discover a small agriturismo in Sicily, about an hour or so outside of Palermo. After e-mailing the owner, *Signor Filippo*, he confirms a spot for the two of us on the day we request. Even though he is Sicilian, he e-mails me in English. "The cooking class is with meat. But if I understand, your sister is vegetarian? Do not worry because we make for her a vegetarian cooking class with no meat, then for you with meat." He is more than happy to agree that we do not cook *pesce*, fish, assuring us that since his agriturismo is inland, and not near the sea, it is impossible to cook seafood that is fresh. "Our politic is to make all fresh." They use the products available to them on short notice.

Signor Filippo's *Agriturismo Tarantola* is on the way to Palermo, our next stop after Agrigento. So our chosen date fits in well with our travel itinerary. The farm is a little off course but basically on the way, and the price is great – only €65, or roughly $85, per person.

When we depart from Agrigento this morning we have no idea that we might completely miss our carefully arranged culinary experience, which is scheduled for eleven o'clock. We leave our hotel by eight thirty since Google Maps indicates that our destination is an hour and a half away. We plan extra time, considering that we have to find this farmhouse in its location in the countryside.

In addition to our Garmin navigator, we have Google Maps with point by point directions on my iPhone. The only problem is that there is no real address for Agriturismo Tarantola. The website just lists it as *Alcamo*, Sicily. Still, Google Maps is able to locate its specific location, so we have confidence to arrive there on time.

The drive starts out as a beautiful scenic tour through southern Sicily; first, along the coast where we see the blue waters of the Mediterranean Sea. As we continue, we begin climbing the higher elevations, and our view is of vineyards, windmills, as well as some dogs guarding sheep.

"Those must be shepherd dogs," says my sister-in-law, who is always happy to see a dog because she misses her Daisy and Cocoa, left behind at home. More interested in the dogs than the sheep, Monica lovingly says, "*Cani*. Those dogs not only protect the sheep but are also used to herd them."

"I like seeing those sheep," I say. "I am not sure but I have a vague memory of hearing that Grandpa Savoca was once a sheepherder." Just that thought and the visual of him standing in a field in Sicily makes me smile.

The pleasant ride unexpectedly becomes a worrisome situation when we are approximately thirty minutes from Alcamo. My iPhone battery is suddenly exhausted, so that is the end of the turn-by-turn directions from Google Maps. As we drive toward Alcamo, we realize that now we are too close to the city and probably nowhere near the agriturismo. Meanwhile the time is ten thirty. I call the agriturismo on my Italian phone to ask for directions and to let Signor Filippo know that we do not know where we are. An English-speaking traveler staying at the agriturismo informs us that we need to input MS 10 as the street address on the navigator. Unfortunately no such road exists according to the Garmin device, only an MS 11. We backtrack and try to locate the right road, but are unable to find any road signs for MS 10 or MS 11. After driving a little longer, we make another call. This time, Signor Filippo himself instructs us to drive to another town, *Camporeale*, and find the correct road from there. "I don't think we'll find the cooking class today," I say.

"Just be patient," Rick suggests. "But you might be right."

I remember seeing a sign for Camporeale, so we follow that road and arrive there at eleven forty. Local residents are walking on the street, so Rick parks the car; I get out and ask a few of them how to find either MS 10 or the agriturismo. None of the people seem to know about this road or Signor Filippo's Agriturismo Tarantola. I am not sure if they even understand my Italian, as they probably speak Sicilian. Fortunately a young Italian woman, who speaks some English, kindly translates to a second woman what my problem is. The second woman then motions to me to follow her in her vehicle. The English-speaking woman explains, "She will drive you to the edge of town and direct you to the right road. Once you are on that road you will find a sign for the agriturismo." God bless these friendly and generous Sicilian women for taking time away from their own agendas to help us.

So we do as we are told and follow behind this woman's car to the road leading out of Camporeale. This road is heading out of town on the opposite side from which we entered. Leaving us at the edge of town, she tells us in Italian or Sicilian to drive past a winery called *Tenuta Rapitala*, Rapitala Estate, and that we will find a sign to

~ 213 ~

where we are headed. I am able to understand a few of her words and say, "*Grazie mille. Buona giornata.*" Thank you very much. Have a nice day. Amazingly, we arrive at Agriturismo Tarantola at noon, only an hour late.

We find Signor Filippo outside to greet us with hugs and kisses. He has his car keys in his hand and he says, "I was just leaving to go out to look for you." Incredible, but this is Sicily! These are real Sicilian people! I feel at home.

A Cooking Class in Sicily

The welcoming Signor Filippo is tall, attractive, and *molto gentile*, very kind. After ushering us inside his cucina we meet *Leno*, the senior chef, and *Giuseppe*, his assistant chef, both of whom are cooking today. A female chef is also working with us, and I believe her name is *Lucrezia*.

This large commercial kitchen sparkles with lots of stainless steel. The counters, the cabinets, the drawers, the refrigerator—all are made of stainless steel, and the look is complete with the multiple ladles hanging from the ceiling. I sense that I am in the right place.

We are preparing several courses, including a traditional Sicilian type of pizza, called *sfincione*, two pasta dishes, one vegetarian and one with meat; eggplant roll-ups, and meat roll-ups, *braciolone*, as well as a dessert known as *cassatelle*. Before we begin cooking, Signor

Filippo offers us a glass of his wine, *Conti Testa Cabernet Syrah*. Not only is Signor Filippo the owner of this agriturismo as well as a 120-hectare wine farm, but he is actually a count, Count Filippo Testa; hence, the name of the wine, Conti Testa. I am honored to be in the presence of nobility here today.

We start by making breadcrumbs and browning them on the stove. The pomodoro sauce is already cooking in a pot on the stove. We then prepare the vegetables to be added to the sauce for the vegetarian pasta. Several processes are happening at once between the three chefs, Monica, and me. Signor Filippo oversees the process.

Braciolone are made with what looks like a thinly-sliced flank steak, which Leno is pounding very flat. He begins to fill them and teaches us his technique of adding pieces of hard-boiled egg, raisins, pine nuts, red onions, pomodoro paste, bread crumbs, and *caciocavallo* cheese. The eggplant roll-ups are filled with the same ingredients as the braciolone except meat. Monica participates in the preparation of the vegan kind, and I fill the meat roll-ups.

"*Scusi, ma che cosa è il caciocavallo?*" I ask, not familiar with this type of cheese. Leno explains to us in Italian that caciocavallo cheese comes from a cow.

Translated, caciocavallo means cheese on horseback. During the aging and curing process the cheese is shaped into a ball, then tied with a rope, and allowed to hang side by side with another ball of cheese. In this way the cheese straddles a horizontal stick and resembles saddlebags used on a horse. Signor Filippo, who is also in and out of the kitchen, helps with the translation and a further explanation. "This cheese is predominantly found in Sicily and southern Italy."

Pecorino cheese is also added to the braciolone. On my own, I would never think to add these ingredients inside a roll-up. The meat roll-ups need to be held together with toothpicks and the eggplant roll-ups as well, although they do not require as many to keep them in one piece.

Giuseppe sautés both the meat- and eggplant roll-ups in olive oil, and we add pomodoro sauce before the cooking is finished. At the same time, Giuseppe is keeping a close eye on several pots which contain pasta and the pomodoro sauce. *Anelli Siciliani* pasta, of the *De Cecco* brand, is pasta shaped like small rings; it is boiling on the stove, and when ready, Giuseppe drains the pasta. We then mix in the prepared ingredients for the meatless entrée. The vegetables include eggplant, peas, and carrots, as wells as breadcrumbs for the top.

In another pan on the stove the *ragu* is cooking in hot olive oil. This ragu consists of ground beef mixed with onions, pomodoro sauce, tomato paste, as well as some white wine. Giuseppe instructs both Monica and me to stir the sauce, and the pasta. Then, after he adds the vegetables and the ragu, we continue mixing what will become the two pasta meals. When ready he pours the pasta into spring form pans and places them into the large commercial oven. So both pastas will be baked dishes today, *pasta al forno.*

Between watching our instructor chefs and listening to directions, neither Monica nor I say much, so as not to miss anything. During all of this activity, I am trying to jot down some notes in the hope of re-creating these dishes in the future. My camera is here too. Occasionally I have a chance to snap some photos, although Rick is in the kitchen for part of this class and helps out with the photos. Since he does not feel well today, he chooses not to walk but to rest inside Agriturismo Tarantola while Monica and I are in class.

Next on today's menu is sfincione, a Sicilian type of rectangular pizza without mozzarella cheese."This sfincione is not what you find on the streets of Palermo," Count Filippo explains, "I know because I lived there. This particular sfincione is specific for this area of Sicily, between Alcamo and Camporeale." I notice once again how the local Italians make sure to mention their region's specialties with great pride.

I am very interested in the making of the sfincione. Leno uses 15 grams of lievito cake yeast to half a kilogram of flour. Then he adds enough water to make the dough very runny and sticky. He allows me to knead it for ten minutes or so, and then sets it aside to rise for twenty minutes. The time to rise is dictated by the weather. On a hot day the time needed for the dough to rise properly might only be ten minutes. After the rising time Chef Leno pours the very wet dough into a rectangular pan, well-greased with fresh green olive oil from Filippo's farm. Monica is involved in adding the toppings; first she adds the pomodoro sauce, then the caciocavallo cheese, the onion, and basil, as well as the bread crumbs. Leno tops all this off with more olive oil. Both Monica and I look at each other, a little surprised to see so much olive oil added to the sfincione. Of course we are thinking about pizza, and neither of us is familiar with making sfincione. Next, our chef carefully places the large pan into the commercial oven to bake the sfincione at two hundred degrees Centigrade, approximately four hundred degrees Fahrenheit for fifteen to twenty minutes. When the dish is done, it looks fantastic. He lifts up one edge of the pizza-like specialty to show us the slightly blackened crust, as if to prove that this is the key to a well-made sfincione.

"Beautiful," I say, and he smiles.

I enjoy Filippo's subtle presence in his kitchen while the chefs manage the hands-on cooking. Filippo shares with us a little background as to how he came to own this wine farm, as he calls it. "At one time I was a jazz musician. After my father died, I had a decision to make, and I chose this path to operate my own wine farm." Tarantola Wine Farm happens to be in full harvest, now that it is mid-September. This harvest lasts two full months, according to Signor Filippo. He explains that for fifty hectares, the grapes are harvested by hand by crews numbering thirty people. Two men operate harvesting machines on the remaining hectares, so at harvest time this is a full-time job. Exuberant when talking about the harvest and the wine, Filippo clearly is passionate about his farm.

Sharing a glass of wine, conversation, and hands-on cooking here already surpasses my expectations of what today might bring. I am so glad to be here.

Leno motions for us to follow him to another counter, because now is the time to prepare the dessert, the cassatelle. He begins to make the dough from white wine, flour, and a little olive oil instead of water. In Italian he tells us that the olive oil makes the pastry dough light.

After kneading for a while, we let the dough sit while we make the filling for these Sicilian treats. The fresh ricotta, delivered this morning by the neighboring farmer, is mixed with sugar at a ratio of one kilogram of ricotta to 400 grams of sugar. Then we add mini chocolate chips. Monica and I observe as Leno rolls a small section of dough until it is flat. He then shows us how to place just the right amount of filling in the center of the pastry dough. We take turns making the cassatelle, one at a time, by folding over the edge and forming a turnover, which is shaped similar to ravioli. With our fingers we seal the edges closed. Then we use a tool to cut around this individual *cassatella*.

Not to waste anything, the remainder of the dough is cut into strips and, along with the cassatelle, these *chiacchiere*, as Filippo calls them, are fried in oil and served with confectioner's sugar. The chiacchiere are commonly served during the Italian festival of *Carnevale*.

After the cooking lesson, Signor Filippo leads us out to the lovely, peaceful terrace where my brother joins us for lunch. The table is set with nine pieces of silverware for each of us on dark green tablecloths. A few cats wander around, looking for a handout. I love the atmosphere and again enjoy eating outside in Sicily.

We indulge in a wonderful meal of way too much food. Afterward Signor Filippo serves us a limoncello, and Leno encourages us to smell the fragrant citronella growing next to the terrace. The grounds are landscaped beautifully. This outdoor experience is one of complete tranquility in the countryside of Sicilia.

"Signor Filippo, we cannot thank you enough. Today has been wonderful," I say as we prepare to leave this peaceful place in the middle of Sicily.

"Yes, we loved it. And the food was delicious," Monica says.

"Thank you for everything. *Ciao*, Giuseppe. *Ciao*, Leno," Rick says, .

"You will have to come back and stay here for a few days," says Filippo.

"*Grazie mille.*"

Count Filippo poses for a final photo with Monica and me, and gives us each a hug. With mixed emotions we walk toward the car to begin our journey toward Palermo, our next stop on this Sicilian adventure.

Our First Two Days in Palermo

Via Ottavio D'Aragona, 25, is the address of our lodging in Palermo, and at 3:30PM we hear the familiar female voice of the GPS instruct us toward our destination.

Residenza D' Aragona is an elegant, early twentieth-century, twenty-room bed-and-breakfast lodging in the historical center of Palermo. This year we have four nights booked here compared with one night during our stay in 2009. I recall how huge the rooms are, because these are converted apartment suites.

Since the reception lobby closes at one in the afternoon, the only way to gain access is to arrange by phone for an agent to meet us and open the door when we reach the premises. At 4:45PM I phone the B&B to inform them of our estimated arrival time of approximately 5:15PM. The kind female voice assures me of her presence to check us into our accommodations.

By 4:45PM we enter the city limits of Palermo, and, as we expect, the traffic is very similar to, if not worse than that of Catania. Palermo is twice the size of Catania, so no surprise that the roads are busy and chaotic. "Idiots on both sides," Rick mutters, as he feels the stress driving on *Via Vittorio Emanuele* in the busy Sicilian city. Sitting in the front passenger seat, Monica acts as a calm co-pilot. Once we turn onto the hectic one-way street, *Via Roma,* Vespas seem to take over the road and weave in and out of lanes of stop-and-go traffic. I observe a woman who is begging in the street at a stop light at the intersection of *Via Cavour* and Via Roma. "We are getting close. I recognize this area. The street we need is off Via Roma," says Monica. By 5:05PM we arrive in front of Residenza D' Aragona, where Rick can temporarily park the car on the street, so we may unload our luggage.

All of us feel some familiarity with this area. We are met by an attractive young Italian woman who is smiling. "*Buona sera,*" she says, as she unlocks the door. "Please come in."

"I'll park the car, while you two check in," Rick says.

"That's right. There's a parking garage just down the street from here, isn't there?" I say. Monica and I handle the check-in process while Rick drives to the parking facility where the car will remain until we leave for the airport four days from now. After the accident and damage to our car in Siracusa, Rick's thoughts on driving are less than enthusiastic. Due to our unanimous decision to park our rental car until we leave Palermo, we agree to walk everywhere or take buses while here. Naturally, Rick likes the plan, but Monica and I are okay with it too.

By seven o'clock we are ready for dinner. "Let's try this place just a few streets over," says Monica as she browses some restaurant recommendations on the back of a map.

"Sounds good. I don't feel like walking too far tonight," I say. We easily find the nearby *Ristorante Il Mirto e la Rosa* on *Via Principe Granatelli*. Not hungry enough for dinner after that food fest this afternoon, I order bruschetta and *tricolore* salad. On the walk back to the hotel, we stop in at a panificio and I buy a bag of ten small Sicilian cookies for one euro. Such a deal.

This morning I have the chance to sleep in and not feel rushed. Our B&B is comfortable and quiet. My room is huge with a queen-size bed, a full-size couch, which converts to a bed, and an entire kitchen unit at an optional added cost of ten euros a day, if a guest chooses to use it. A large wardrobe serves as a closet; a flat-screen TV, and a desk complete the main room. The bathroom is very modern, an important aspect for me. I dislike old plumbing in hotels.

After our preferred breakfast of yogurt, fruit, and cappuccino, the three of us buy tickets from the receptionist for the hop-on-hop-off sightseeing bus. The cost is €20 for a 24-hour ticket and I decide to pay the extra €5 to have the option to visit *Monreale*, home to the twelfth-century cathedral, which is famous for its extensive Byzantine mosaics. Since Rick and Monica are not interested, I intend to go there by myself tomorrow.

"The bus stop isn't too far from here," Rick says, as he looks at the map. "Let's walk there and hope that we can make the first bus." After a short wait, the tour bus arrives a few blocks away from our hotel. Unfortunately for us, the open-air second level is already filled with passengers, so we take our seats on the lower level. This turns out to be a poor choice for sightseeing or taking photos. So, as soon as the opportunity arises and seats become available atop, Monica and I climb the stairs and sit on the second level, which provides us with a much better perspective. We are seeing quite a bit of the city while learning about Palermo through the headsets provided. Something new I hear is that Palermo has an English Garden.

After the bus ride, we continue to explore the city on foot and arrive at the Palermo market, a vibrant scene. Stall after stall with some of the most beautiful fruits and vegetables provide another photo op for me and also a chance to buy a banana for a snack later. Crowds of people wander between the various vendors, most of whom seem to be Italian. We pass by several fresh fish- as well as butcher stalls and also some with non-food items, such as DVDs, purses, clothing, cell phone cases, and jewelry for sale.

Palermo appears to be much cleaner than Catania. The people here seem to dress with a little more sense of fashion. After all, Palermo is the capital of Sicily, so I should not be surprised.

As we continue our stroll, we come upon the shop of *Gino Conciauro*, the shoemaker we know from our previous trip. We recognize his painted white shop with red lettering, and the outside racks displaying men's leather shoes for sale.

Not seeing the friendly Gino, we ask another gentleman inside the shop about him. "*Dove è Gino? Siamo Americani. Siamo venuti qui due anni fa e ha mandato cartoline da Florida e South Carolina.*" Where is Gino? We are Americans. We came here two years ago and later sent postcards from Florida and South Carolina.

The grey-haired gentleman smiles and now seems to understand. He leads us to the wall of postcards on display. Together we locate the two cards, to prove our point. Now he smiles even more and introduces himself as *Salvatore*. He explains that he is Gino's son, and that Gino is not here. We are disappointed not to see Gino, but we meet another man, *Agostino,* who explains that he too is Gino's son.

I am a little confused because these men do not look young enough to be Gino's sons. I would estimate Gino to be fifty years old, and these men look that age themselves. I am not sure they understand that much English, so maybe we have a misunderstanding. When I ask how old their father is, they tell me, "*Ottanta anni,*" eighty years old.

I turn to Monica and say, "I wonder if there really is a father named Gino. I can't believe that the one we met is that old. But maybe he really is eighty and looks much younger."

"I don't remember Gino being that old," says Monica.

"Too bad," Rick says. "I wish he were here."

Salvatore generously offers us some water and gives us a liter of *acqua naturale* with some clear plastic cups. Since the weather is very hot, we appreciate the gesture and accept his hospitality with a *"Grazie mille."*

"How nice of him to offer us this water. I am really thirsty," I say.

"Yes, he is very nice," says Monica.

Salvatore allows us to go inside and watch the two shoemakers at work. "*Mi permette di scattare alcune foto?*" Permission to take photos? Salvatore nods approval. I am grateful for the opportunity, because everything looks very old-fashioned, an Old World setting. The shoemakers themselves appear pleased and are willing to pose for a few photos. The men's leather shoes cost much more this time, 98€ compared with the price of 30€ two years ago.

Across the street, we recognize the old closed-down church from the last visit; I think it is permanently closed. How sad that some of the churches are no longer open. We continue sightseeing, and soon arrive in front of Palermo's famous nineteenth-century opera house, *Teatro Massimo*, remembered by film lovers for the final scene from *The Godfather*. The neoclassical architecture amazes me, even though today is not the first time I see this landmark with its Greek-style columns and bronze sculptured lions,.

We also notice *Rossopomodoro*, the now-closed restaurant,. We are familiar with this name as part of a chain of restaurants with former locations in the States. I guess economic hard times force this business to close here as well. I am both sad and disappointed.

"By the way, we need to do our laundry," I say to Monica.

"I saw a place while we were riding the bus. I think it was on *Via Volturno*, not too far away." I can always count on my sister-in-law's resourcefulness in finding restaurants and other points of interest. "Do you want to walk there now so we can check the hours that they are open?" Monica says.

"Sure. And I want to find a pasticceria that sells cannoli. I haven't had any since we arrived in Sicily, and Palermo is supposed to have the best cannoli," I say. So we make our way to *L'Oblo*, the self-service laundromat at *Via Volturno*, 62.

Pleasantly surprised to discover that this *lavanderia a gettoni* is open during the afternoon, we walk inside. The place is spotless and the air is filled with the clean scent of detergent. "*Buongiorno*," I say to the friendly, English-speaking woman who runs the laundromat. She verifies the hours of operation. "Yes, we are open today until seven thirty. Tomorrow is Saturday, and we close at two thirty."

"*Grazie, signora.* We'll be back later," I say. Monica and I like the later hours and decide to return some time before dinner.

With temperatures in the seventies and low eighties, the weather here is comfortable. People are dressed casually, no scarves or stiletto heels here, but they do not appear sloppy. Since it is so warm, I am wearing shorts and short sleeves most days. This is the first time in Italy that I do not wear long pants each day, but I am glad I can be comfortable.

I like being in Palermo and having time to enjoy this Sicilian city of six hundred thousand people.

Close to four-thirty Rick, Monica, and I leave the hotel pulling our rolling luggage filled with our dirty laundry. In less than ten minutes we arrive at L'Oblo to find the same pleasant woman willing to help us operate the machines. The cost for the washer is 4€ for thirty-five minutes and the cost for the dryer is 2€ for twenty minutes. We deposit our laundry in the machines, and Rick agrees to wait with the empty luggage while Monica and I use the time to do some quick shopping. "I need to go to that farmacia we passed, so I can buy some Hall's cough drops and Vitamin C. Rick and I have sore throats," Monica says.

"Okay, and I want to return to the ceramics shop of *Enzo Scerrino*, whose hand-painted designs I admired earlier," I say.

His shop is close by so I reach it in five minutes. The artist, who is also the owner, shakes his head when I ask for the Trinacria pieces, which are no longer on display. "*Mi dispiace, li ho venduto, signora.*" He apologizes and informs me that the Trinacria design piece I like is sold out.

So I purchase a mug painted in navy blue, with golden, ochre, and white flowers. For 10€ the price is affordable. "*Grazie, signore,*" I say as I exit his shop.

I recall that a pasticceria is on the corner of this street. I buy three small cannoli at the cost of 1€ apiece, and then head back toward the laundromat, meeting up with Monica along the way.

We arrive back at the laundry in time to unload the washers and insert the wet clothing into the dryers. Rick is reading a magazine, and, while we wait, I have a chance to converse with the woman who tells me she is the owner. "Your laundromat is so clean and I am happy you have afternoon hours, something unusual in Italy."

"Thank you," she replies. "When I first came here, mine was the only laundry."

"You speak such good English. Did you spend time in the States?" I ask.

"Yes," she says. "I lived in Massachusetts for a while."

No wonder she speaks such good English, I think. She seems like a nice lady, as well as a good business woman.

Before our clothes are finished drying, an Italian woman enters with her laundry. She is accompanied by a young man. He appears to be seventeen or eighteen years old, and I assume he is her son. Once he starts talking on his cell phone, this woman's behavior startles me. She yells at him in Sicilian, and I feel embarrassed for him. Trying to ignore the scene, I check the dryer, retrieve my clean clothing, and quickly begin to fold my clothes. As soon as Monica and I complete our business here, we leave with Rick, pulling our luggage filled with fresh-smelling clothes.

On the street, I see the arguing woman sitting in a car; she is still gesturing at this young man. What a complete contrast: the laundry owner and her customer.

A short rest at our hotel seems like a good idea. Afterward, Monica, Rick, and I meet at seven o'clock to leave for dinner. "Rick and I found this cozy outdoor place for dinner. It looks nice," Monica says, "I think you'll like it." *Trattoria A' Cuccagna*, on *Via Principe di Granatelli* is a short walk from our hotel, and while the restaurant also offers indoor seating, we like the outdoor atmosphere. Unfortunately the service is not as good as the food, but the meal and ambience make up for it. My gnocchi with caciocavallo cheese and insalata mista tastes just right. I do not need to order dessert because I plan on eating one of the cannoli sitting in my refrigerator at the hotel. Just the thought of it makes my mouth water.

Cathedrals and Churches

I am on my own today to go to Monreale, the small town on top of a hill just eight kilometers outside Palermo. Monreale is the location of the famous twelfth-century Norman cathedral, *Monreale di Duomo*, known mostly for its interior golden mosaics.

I board the hop-on-hop-off bus to my destination, but once seated, I realize that I do not have my receipt from yesterday, which indicates the time and date stamp. My first concern is that the young lady checking tickets is going to force me to leave, but she kindly smiles and gives me a break, another example of the friendly Sicilian people. The ride to this hilltop town takes almost an hour because the bus makes multiple stops to load and unload passengers.

Once I arrive in Monreale, I take note of my surroundings, as is my habit, and take a photo of a landmark to help me return to the same location when I am ready to leave. From here the view of the *Conca d' Oro* valley below is incredible. I am able to see all the way down to the sea and much of Palermo, as well as the surrounding countryside.

Just a few blocks away from the bus stop I am in the center of town, the *Piazza Vittorio Emanuele,* where I look at a church, that I think is probably the Duomo; yet the façade, which I am facing, is not so impressive.

After a local Sicilian verifies that this building is indeed the cathedral, I walk around the building to its main entrance in *Piazza Guglielmo II.* This entrance is much more what I expect of a cathedral.

Crowds of well-dressed Italians fill the piazza in front of the cathedral, and I realize that a wedding is about to take place. How fascinating!

I note the time to be 10:40AM and assume that the wedding probably begins at 11:00AM. I am worried that I may not be allowed inside. I feel excited to be here to witness the flurry of activity in the piazza as wedding guests wait to enter the church. But I also feel anxious that I have a limited amount of time to visit the inside of the Duomo.

Maybe if I hurry, I might at least have the opportunity to see some of the interior mosaics. Some wedding guests, as well as visitors like me, are entering the cathedral through the two huge Romanesque bronze front doors. I see no security personnel keeping tourists out right now. I enter with the others and notice the elaborate floral wedding decorations of pink and white roses attached to the pews. Simply gorgeous.

The cathedral is immense, and almost immediately I am struck by the beauty of the mosaics throughout the church: the ceiling, the altar, and the walls. The intricate designs are stunning and I feel a sense of urgency to capture this scene quickly with my camera. So I make my way around this magnificent cathedral, marveling in amazement, and snapping photos with my Nikon digital camera.

Although the ceiling is made of wood, it appears to also be covered in mosaics. I remember reading some statistics from Frommer's about these mosaics: More than sixty-eight thousand square feet are covered with stunning mosaics, which utilize almost five thousand pounds of gold. What seems incredible is that over one hundred and thirty individual mosaics adorn this building. The mosaics here are considered to be surpassed only by those in the *Basilica Saint Sofia* in Istanbul.

The central figure to which my eyes gravitate is the half-figure of Christ the Pantocrator in gold mosaics at the central apse: not only beautiful but also a huge work of art. I am reminded of the mosaics and the same Pantocrator figure of Christ in the Cefalù cathedral. Monreale's cathedral, however, is much larger. Because the interior of this cathedral is so huge, it is hard to appreciate the immensity of the figure of Christ. It measures forty-two feet across and thirty feet high. Awesome.

The bells begin to toll; it is 11:00AM, so I know I must leave. What an added treat to see the beautiful bride at the church entrance with her proud father. As I listen to the sounds of the organ playing the traditional *Wedding March* and witness the slow walk down the aisle, I am filled with emotion and have tears of happiness in my eyes.

Since I am in Monreale with time to spare, I decide to visit the Benedictine Cloister in the same piazza next to the cathedral. The entrance fee of six euros is reasonable and the line is short. Here I am treated to another beautiful example of Sicilian architecture, clearly with an Arab influence. The building is shaped like a rectangle with an inner courtyard or quadrangle.

Two hundred twenty-eight twin columns surround this courtyard; what is particularly interesting about the carved columns is that no two are alike. Frescoes on the walls are an added surprise as I wander through this cloister. My self-guided tour here is well worth the time.

Before I leave this hilltop town, I make a stop to use the very clean public restrooms for a fee of fifty euro cents. Afterward, on the walk back toward the bus stop, I am surprised to find a trio of young teen boys singing. They seem happy but when I ask permission to record them, they laugh but shake their heads and immediately stop singing. "We are not good singers," they say.

I think they sound great but respect their wishes. "*Bravo. Grazie. Buona giornata.*" Good, thank you. Have a nice day. Their happy voices and smiling faces are a Monreale memory I cherish.

A short stop at the *Montereale Cafè* near the bus stop is a great place for a light lunch – bruschetta pomodoro and gelato. *Perfetto.* This really is the name of the café. Monreale is a contraction for the name Montereale, which means royal mountain.

I must be on the 12:30PM bus back to Palermo because the hotel receptionist leaves at 2:00PM today and I need to pay my bill. We plan to check out very early Monday morning, and since tomorrow is Sunday when no one is working, today is my only opportunity to settle the final bill. I arrive back at 1:30PM promptly and complete my paperwork with the hotel clerk. Rick and Monica appear to be out, so I take advantage of some free time to catch up on e-mail while I relax in my quiet room.

An hour later I am back on the street with no particular plan. Noticing a fruit vendor, I buy a banana. I am also in the mood for a panini. The *negozio di alimentari*, grocery store, however, is closed for the afternoon until 4:30PM.

The docks are just a few blocks from here, so I head in that direction. I am in luck when I see a corner building with outdoor tables that are occupied. "Great," I say to myself, "something is open." *Ganci Gelateria* is exactly what I need, and I go inside to check out the flavors of gelato. For the unbelievably low price of €1.70 I walk out carrying a cone with two scoops of gelato, one pistachio and one *stracciatella*, chocolate chip. As an added treat a pizzelle cookie tops off the gelato.

Curious to see the docks up close, I cross the street while I enjoy this cool treat and walk toward the water. The docks are fenced off with guards standing duty, but no one stops me from walking all the way to the water's edge. The *Grand Celebration* cruise ship is in port along with a ferry from the *Tirrenia* line. This ferry transports passengers between Naples and Palermo, and I understand that the crossing takes ten hours. I prefer the one-hour flight on which we have reservations for Monday.

The cruise ship looks somewhat familiar; I notice the tell-tale funnel shaped like a whale tail, Carnival Cruise line's trademark. The ship's funnel is now painted blue, but this is the original *Carnival Celebration* cruise ship. These days the ship sails to Greece, Brazil, Malta, Venice, and other ports in the Mediterranean.

After shooting some photos along the dock, I amble back to the port entrance where I notice a few souvenir shops. A man driving a horse-drawn carriage catches my attention when he shouts to me something about a ride for €30. Although I can't hear him well, I shake my head and keep moving.

After I return to my room, Monica phones. "Hi, Rick and I are back and we would like to go out to find a supermercato so Rick can buy some M&M's." Yes, the exercise is directly tied to chocolate consumption, but that story is for another book. We agree to leave at six o'clock.

While we are out looking for a supermarket, we find ourselves in the midst of a major *la passeggiata*, the daily ritual of an early evening stroll. On this Saturday evening the large piazza through which we pass is filled with people, and a live band is playing. Food vendors are setting up, and it seems that the residents are observing some type of festivity. My interest is piqued; I want to know what is happening. Rick, however, has an agenda and dislikes the noise, so he is not amused. Not finding any store to buy the M&M's, I enlist the aid of an Italian couple who are walking alongside us. *"Per favore, sapete dove c'è un supermercato?"* Please, do you know where there is a supermarket?

Without hesitation the friendly woman points down the street and informs us that within a block or so we will find it. I am grateful because Rick's patience is wearing thin and he is almost ready to turn around and walk back to the hotel. The directions are perfect, and we see the store within the next few minutes. Thank goodness, M&M's are available here, and Rick's mission is accomplished. Monica buys some bottles of water, and we walk back to the hotel.

Rick cannot move fast enough to avoid the noises of the city on a weekend.

After dropping off the purchases in the hotel we head out for dinner. A small outdoor restaurant advertising authentic Sicilian food is our destination. *La Ducchessa Pizzeria* is conveniently located just off Via Roma on a quiet side street near the hotel. Quiet is the goal for the evening, so this seems perfect.

Anxious to try the Sicilian pizza, I ask the young waitress to explain the difference between traditional and Sicilian pizza. I think that I already know the difference to be related to the thicknesss of the crust. She surprises me, though, with her answer. "Sicilian pizza is made with the fresh ingredients from our region, so it is made with tomatoes, arugula, as well as mozzarella and ricotta cheese," she says in perfect English.

"That sounds good. I think I'll order that," I say. My decision turns out to be a good one since the pizza tastes delicious. The tomatoes are the small cherry tomatoes and the crust is thin. A light layer of tomato sauce tops the pizza.

"Monica, you always find the best restaurants. I'm glad we came here," I say.

"I happened to see the sign earlier while we were out walking past here, and the side street seemed like a quiet place for dinner."

"You were right. I'm glad I was able to try some authentic cuisine from the region. And of course, since I am in Palermo, I can't pass up cannoli for dessert. Sicily definitely has the best cannoli," I say.

On my last full day in Sicily I am in no hurry to get moving, so I lie awake in my bed for a while, reliving our days here. Hmm, I think, I might as well jot down these memories for future reference. And so I write: "Even without using the car, I have enjoyed Palermo and Monreale. I would have liked to visit *Erice* and *Trapani*, but I think it would have felt rushed, so I have no regrets. Besides, I know I will be back one day."

Today is yet another warm, sunny day, so Rick and I walk to the nearby parking garage to pay the bill and make arrangements to retrieve the vehicle tomorrow morning. The attendant reassures us that all we need to do is ring the bell and someone will have the car ready. They are open twenty-four hours.

"I'm glad we came and double-checked everything. It would be a nightmare if we couldn't get the car and miss our early flight to the mainland tomorrow, " I say to my brother.

"Yeah, they seem pretty nice here. I'm glad, too, we stopped by now."

Back at the hotel, Monica waits for us, ready to venture outside to explore more of Palermo. The plan is to visit the cathedral, which is one of the most recognized landmarks in the city. What makes this structure so unique is its mix of different architectural styles. Due to multiple rebuilding projects the Duomo features designs of Norman, Gothic, Byzantine, Arab, Swabian (from Germany), romanesque, and baroque influences. Construction of the *Cattedrale di Palermo*, Palermo Cathedral dates back to the twelfth century over the original site of a Roman temple. *Best of Sicily Magazine* discusses the cathedral's history, mentioned in Arab records from the year 831. Much is unknown; however, a Christian basilica, and later a mosque are two religious buildings that pre-date the current cathedral.

What strikes me first upon seeing the cathedral from *Piazza di Cattedrale* are its immense size and green dome.

Surrounded by palm trees, this beautiful building makes a majestic impression. Rick enjoys walking about the site, examining the various architectural aspects of the cathedral.

Quite a few people are in the piazza as Mass will likely be starting soon. Like in Monreale, I move to the entrance quickly, to take advantage of the opportunity to view the interior and shoot some photos. Once the service begins, out of respect, no photos are allowed.

The inside of the cathedral is equally as magnificent to me as the view of the exterior. In shades of white and gold, elegance and beauty describe this large place of worship and its clearly baroque style. Its ceiling is arched and painted with intricate geometric patterns above the long nave, which is punctuated by white columns connected by arches. High on the columns sit statues of the saints on decorative pedestals. Lower down on each column and slightly to the side, gold sconces hold multiple lights, which appear as white candles.

On the arched domed ceiling over the front altar I see a beautiful painting of angels and clouds. Along the side aisles many elaborately-designed marble altars line the walls. I stop to photograph one of the large wooden confessionals near the front of the church. Italy has so many beautiful churches, but this is certainly one of the most impressive.

As we make our way back toward the hotel, Rick and Monica motion for me to follow them into an interesting church they notice. Today is Sunday, so entering yet another place of worship is probably appropriate. Not sure what the attraction is from the outside, except that the entrance door is open, I follow them up five or six steps into another stunning chiesa. *Chiesa di San Matteo* is unassuming from the exterior but once inside, I marvel at the gorgeous sight. The entire arched ceiling consists of colorful frescoes, which continue onto the upper portions of the arches above the four rows of columns. Marble floors in shades of rose, grey, white, and gold add to the richness of this seventeenth-century baroque church. Absolutely stunning.

Not far from here we reach the *Quattro Canti*, probably the most famous intersection of Palermo. Situated where *Corso Vittorio Emanuele* meets *Via Maqueda*, this place is actually *Piazza Vigilena*, but the residents of Palermo call it Quattro Canti, meaning four corners. Four separate three-story baroque buildings with sculptures on their façades, occupy this intersection, which is considered the traditional center of Palermo.

After a morning of sightseeing we decide to stop for something cool to drink at a trattoria on *Via Bara All' Olivetta*, a small pedestrian street near Teatro Massimo. While the three of us are sitting at an outside table, a woman with a dog on a leash sits down at the next table. "Hi, puppy," Monica says lovingly, obviously pleased to see the dog. Missing her own two cani, Daisy and Cocoa, Monica smiles at the woman. "What a beautiful dog. How old is she?"

The lady smiles and responds in a German accent. She seems pleasant and speaks excellent English. The three of us are eager to have a conversation in English so we spend some time discussing various topics with her. "I have lived here for twenty-six years. I married a Sicilian man." We talk about life in Sicily and I am interested in her perspective on the job situation and the government here.

"What do you find to be the biggest difference between here and Germany?" I ask.

She laughs and without hesitation, says, "The organization." We all laugh and continue to enjoy the camaraderie we feel with someone who lives here, yet is not Sicilian herself.

After we finish our drinks, Rick and Monica are ready to go back to the hotel and relax. I am not tired and feel ready to do something. "The Teatro Massimo is on the next street and I think they have tours. If they are open today, I'd like to see if I can take a tour. I'll see you later at the hotel."

"Okay, I think we are going to rest. We still don't feel good and a nap sounds like a plan," says Monica.

"See you later. *Ciao*."

I wave goodbye as I leave to walk to Teatro Massimo, and hope the theater has Sunday hours. As I reach the end of the street, I can see the theater across the busy *Via Maqueda*. My heart is light as I see the open doors and some visitors walking up the steps and into the theater. How exciting! I am going to tour this famous Palermo landmark.

A Tour of Teatro Massimo

I feel psyched to be doing something on my own in Sicily again. As I walk up the theater's massive steps I hope that tickets are still available for today. I will be disappointed if they are sold out.

I know that Teatro Massimo has the largest stage in Italy and is renowned for perfect acoustics, but I expect to learn more. Just the thought of being inside this historic theater thrills me. I do not see that many people in the lobby and I am delighted that I can purchase a ticket for 8€ and join a tour conducted in English and starting soon. Perfetto!

A young enthusiastic Italian woman named Rachel is the guide of our small tour group of five people. Her English is excellent as I assume it would have to be in order to conduct tours for American and other English-speaking visitors. The first place we visit is the grand lobby, which immediately impresses me with its extremely high ceilings, glass chandeliers, marble columns, and velvet draperies. Vintage costumes from previous operas are displayed in this area. "You may take photos in here, but once inside the auditorium, no photos are allowed," our guide informs us. I take advantage of this opportunity before she directs us toward the auditorium for the next phase of the tour.

As soon as I enter the richly decorated theater, I sense that I am standing in a place of fame. Its rich decor in shades of gold and red is appealing even in an almost-empty theater. "Although Teatro Massimo was built in 1875, there was a period of twenty-three years when the theater had been closed. It finally re-opened in 1997. Almost everything inside is original, including the Murano glass lighting fixtures on the walls. The refurbished red velvet seats are an exception," Rachel says.

I wish I could photograph the interior but I abide by the rules. I am a little surprised, especially since we are on a tour rather than at a performance. The guide continues with some interesting statistics. "This is the largest stage in Italy and third largest in Europe, with dimensions of fifty meters in height, forty meters in depth, and thirty meters across. The stage is larger than the seating area of the auditorium."

I learn that the seats on the ground level are called stalls, and above them are five levels of balconies. The sixth level is called the gallery. "At one time this auditorium could accommodate 3,000 people, but present regulations allow for a seating capacity of 1,350. May I point out that Teatro Massimo's acoustics are considered the best in Europe," Rachel says with pride.

Another unique feature is a domed ceiling comprised of eleven artistically painted panels, which can be opened on warm evenings for ventilation. They operate on a system of rollers inside the dome. What a practical idea before the era of climate-controlled venues. Although the theater now is equipped with more features, the air-conditioner is not used during an opera because it can interfere with the singer's voices.

"Next we are going upstairs where I will show you something special." Our tour guide leads us to one of the salons or boxes in the balcony. "This is the Royal Box; it holds twenty-seven seats, rather than six. This special box is usually reserved for VIP's, government officials, and celebrities. Al Pacino actually sat in this seat while he was here filming *Godfather III*," she explains. "Anyone can buy a seat here. The cost is €100 each, but you must be prepared to pay for all twenty-seven seats."

I am impressed and try to imagine Al Pacino sitting here during an opera, or the filming of one. Later I learn that this is not actually the filming location for the opera scenes in *Godfather III* because of the theater closure from 1974 until 1997. The movie's 1990 release makes it clear that one cannot shoot interior scenes inside a closed Teatro Massimo. Instead, the soundstage at Cinecittà Studios in Rome is the real set for those scenes, according to *Franco Sciannameo*, author of *Nino Rota's The Godfather Trilogy: A Film Score Guide*.

While our group walks toward another area of the theater outside of the auditorium, I can hear one of the male opera singers rehearsing for tonight's performance of *The Barber of Seville*. What a thrill for me to listen to that strong baritone voice. "The theater employs its own orchestra and chorus, but the lead roles are sung by famous touring opera singers," Rachel explains.

"We are now going into the Echo Room." I wonder what an echo room is; once inside this circular room I am even more curious. "This is not commonly found in opera houses," our guide says. "This room is unique in that no conversations can be overheard from any place in the room, allowing for privacy. If one stands in the middle and speaks, however, the words are clearly communicated to all areas of the room. "Try it," she says, and each of us takes a turn standing in the center and performing this simple exercise. Amazing.

At the end of the thirty-minute tour, my knowledgeable tour guide informs our small group that tickets may still be available for tonight's performance of *The Barber of Seville*, in case any of us are interested in attending. I am tempted to go; in fact I would love to go, but my first thought is that I have no dressy clothing with me. When I voice my concerns, Rachel dispels any worry regarding appearance. "That is not a problem. You only need to wear dressier clothing if you are sitting in stalls on the lower level. For the balconies or the gallery you can dress more casually. What you are wearing now is fine."

I am surprised to hear this and happy too, even a little excited. My mind is racing. "I've never been to an opera yet have always wanted to attend." The idea of going to my first opera in Italy thrills me.

I hope the prices are reasonable and that a seat for tonight is available. I walk to the entrance of the theater and find the box office where a sign indicates the upcoming events. *The Barber of Seville* is listed for tonight but no prices. After I wait in a short line I ask the ticket seller behind the window to check prices and available seating locations for tonight's performance. Although I can buy a ticket for a seat in the gallery for €20, or one in an upper-level balcony for €40, I decide to buy a ticket for €85, which places me in the first balcony, just left of center. "This is a good seat," the woman says. I am grateful she speaks English. "You will be in a box with two rows of three seats, six total. Your seat is the first one in the second row of the box." This seems a little confusing, since my experience with theater balconies consists of long rows of seats, not individual boxes. I think that sitting in a box is special. Of course I do not realize that this type of seating is typical for an opera performance.

The opera is scheduled to begin at 5:30PM and she advises me to arrive an hour early. "Thank you very much. *Buona sera*," I say.

As I walk back toward my hotel. I'm smiling and thinking about what I am going to wear. I know that Rick and Monica will not care that I have plans for the evening, since neither of them is interested in opera.

I'm hungry and know I will not have time to sit down and eat a meal before the performance. No restaurants are open now, at two thirty in the afternoon. Sometimes the hours for panificios and pasticcerias are different, though, from restaurants and grocery stores. But I remember a pasticceria near the hotel. I'll try that one, I think.

Since the door is open, I go inside and recognize the same friendly girl behind the counter from my earlier visit. *"Scusa, voglio comprare un panino. Potete aiutarmi, per favore?"* Excuse me, I want to buy a panini. Can you help me, please?

"Volete panini? Possiamo fare qui per voi. Prosciutto." You want panini? We can make it here for you. Prosciutto.

I don't know why I am surprised that they can make a panini here for me, but I am thrilled to hear it. *"Si, grazie, prosciutto. E anche tre biscotti pignoli, per favore."* Yes, thank you, prosciutto. And also three pignoli cookies, please.

Satisfied, I walk back to my hotel and enjoy my freshly-prepared meal along with a Coca Light from my refrigerator. Delicioso.

A phone call to my brother's room confirms that he and Monica are not in, so I pen a quick note explaining that I will not be joining them for dinner because I am attending an opera. Won't they be surprised? I have just enough time to freshen up and put on something a bit dressier before I must leave for Teatro Massimo. I can feel the excitement. I am going to the opera!

My First Opera Experience

As I walk out of my B&B, Residenza D'Aragona, wearing my black and white dressy blouse, black pants, my black flats, and sunglasses, I feel on top of the world. I am so happy to have the opportunity to attend my first opera, and even happier that it happens to be in Sicily. The walk to Teatro Massimo takes only ten minutes and I enjoy every step of it, especially because I feel I am dressed nicer than most times I am out for a walk here. Although it is warm today in Palermo, my gold-colored scarf draped across my shoulders is the perfect accessory to wear to the opera. Fashion comes first tonight.

When I arrive at the theater, the doors are closed. Not too many patrons are waiting on the steps, so the emphasis on coming early is a bit exaggerated. I would rather be early than late, however, so I do not mind. I know that once a performance begins, frequently the auditorium doors are closed and no entrance is allowed until the intermission. Perhaps this is the reason for the warning to arrive early. After standing outside nearly thirty minutes, I notice the security personnel opening the doors and allowing the patrons to enter. One of the male ushers checks my ticket and then shows me to my box, or to my room, I should say. The balconies consist of individual small rooms with six chairs, reminiscent of what I know from the movies. I am the first one here in my particular box, and my view of the stage is perfect.

I like that I am early when hardly any seats are occupied, which gives me the chance to observe the décor and furnishings with more attention. In my box, the edge of the wall is adorned with gold-painted wood trim, and I notice that it needs some attention. Close up, I can tell that the rich materials are old and somewhat worn. I recall the tour guide mentioning that this theater is owned partly by the city of Palermo and partly by private owners. Like in many cities throughout the world, funding for the arts is limited, and donations are usually welcomed.

Because of the tour guide's earlier warning against photography inside the auditorium, I do not have my Nikon camera with me; it is in my hotel room. I assume this rule holds true for tonight too, yet I notice many other theatergoers taking photos, both with cameras and camera phones. Although ushers are within the auditorium, none of them seem to mind. Now I regret taking only my iPhone camera with me. At least this is better than not having any camera at all. I make the most of the opportunity and start to photograph various aspects of the theater. Because no other patrons are yet seated in my box, I am able to move about this room and capture different camera angles before the performance begins.

The interior is magnificent with its heavy velvet mahogany curtains, gold-colored walls, and exquisite glass chandeliers. I study the chandeliers closely to see if I can recognize that the glass is the Murano style. I vividly recall my visit to the Schiavon glass factory and showroom in Murano during my last trip to Venice. I know that attention to detail is what creates such high quality in Murano glass. Murano glass products are unique; no two pieces are alike because they are hand-made. They likely have a texture, which is slightly uneven. Minute bubbles may appear just beneath the surface of the glass. The chandeliers appear to be old, and, according to Rachel, they are the original lighting fixtures.

As more people enter and take their seats, I notice that many of the ladies are fanning themselves with hand-held folding fans. Although I do not feel hot, I assume that these women need the fans to stay comfortable since air-conditioning is not in use. Soon three people enter my room, and take their seats in front of me. The two women are accompanied by a man and all three are speaking Italian. They acknowledge me with a nod. "*Buona sera*," I say, and after a reply of buona sera, no further conversation continues between us. The two red velvet, cushioned seats next to me remain vacant the rest of the evening.

A few minutes after the scheduled time for the performance to begin, the house lights dim and the noise level drops. The orchestra conductor turns to face the audience who applaud. I am surprised by his attire; expecting a tuxedo, I notice that he wears a black T-shirt beneath a jacket. After he acknowledges the applause he turns to face the musicians, and the performance begins while the stage curtain is still down. Clearly the music is one of the most important aspects to this production. The moment I hear the first sounds from the live orchestra I recognize the opening sequence immediately and am enthralled. Rossini's Overture from *The Barber of Seville* is one I remember falling asleep to many nights as a child, growing up in a home with classical music playing on the hi-fi in the evening..

Soon the curtain rises and costumed performers are onstage much like they are during a Broadway play. As I watch the performance, I am fascinated. Not until this experience do I fully realize that an opera is much like a play, with actors and a storyline. In operas, though, the dialogues are sung, not spoken, and the music and libretto are more of the driving force than the acting. It does not matter that the opera is in a language other than my native language; the music and voices of the opera singers are powerful enough to convey what is happening.

I am, however, grateful for the chance to research the storyline prior to coming to the theater, so that I am now able to follow the performance and understand what I am seeing and hearing onstage. High above the audience Italian libretto continually updates on a screen. With my fair knowledge of the Italian language I understand much of the performance. According to my program, *The Barber of Seville* is actually an opera buffa, which is a comic opera about everyday people. I recall the tour guide mentioning that this particular opera is a good choice for a novice like me, because the story is a light-hearted one. Such an awesome experience; I am thrilled to be here.

After two hours go by, the intermission takes place. Two of the people in front of me leave and the older woman stays. I am surprised when she speaks to me in English. "Are you enjoying this?"

"Yes, very much. This is my first opera."

"We come here often," she says.

"This is a beautiful theater. I don't see any place here to get a drink, though. Is there a bar here?" I ask.

"Yes, downstairs," she says. I am happy for the light conversation with this woman.

I decide to stay in my seat so as not to risk being late when the curtain goes up, but I could use something to drink. I will have to wait until later. After a twenty-minute intermission, the house lights dim again and the second act begins. Although the stage makes use of several sets, they are simplified and in no way compare to sets from a Broadway theater performance. I do not know the reason.

For the next hour I am completely captivated by the arias and the entire performance. The performers do not use microphones, and I have no problem hearing their trained voices. What a workout for them. And what a terrific performance for the audience.

As I leave the theater with the other patrons and walk down the steps to a brightly lit street that is filled with people, I feel inspired by the Muse and energized by this rich cultural experience. I can say that I am now hooked and looking forward to my next opera event. I may even bring one of those folding fans.

Last Hours in Sicily

With less than three hours of sleep, I awaken to the sound of the alarm on my phone at 3:45AM. I know I have to get out of bed now to be ready to leave for the Palermo airport by 4:30AM. There, we need to allow enough time to return the rental car and catch the 7:00AM flight to Napoli.

Rick, Monica, and I meet in the hotel lobby, which is silent and dark at this early hour. With minimal conversation, we drop our room keys into the designated box and then exit the hotel for the final time on this trip. "I'll go get the car while you wait here with the bags," Rick says before he walks down the street to the parking garage.

"I am so tired," I say to Monica

"I know. Me too."

Within a few minutes Rick pulls up with the Alpha Romeo in front of the hotel and then gets out to help load the bags into the car. My luggage goes into the back seat because it doesn't fit in the trunk. Once we are all inside the car, Rick says, "Okay, Margie, I need the GPS."

For a moment I do not remember where it is, but after a minute I recall that the navigator is packed away inside my bags. "Oh, oh," I say, "I packed it in the luggage. I'll get it. I remember where I put it." I am out of the car without delay and drag the suitcase onto the sidewalk to open it and find the GPS device. Aware of the time and the need to arrive at the airport on time, I feel anxious and stupid at the same time. How dumb is that, Margie, I think, as I sort through the contents of my bag as fast as I can. "I have it. Should I program it for the airport?"

"Yes, that would be great," Rick says. Within a few minutes, and thanks to the GPS, we are on our way to the Palermo airport, known as *Punta Raisi* Airport. The drive through the city at four o'clock in the morning with minimal traffic is a much different experience from the busy daytime chaos on the streets of Palermo.

Once we arrive at the rental car location next to the airport, we pull into a parking space, which we hope draws the least attention to the damaged right fender. The rental car return office is not yet open, so we deposit the keys and documents into the marked drop box. "Let's hope that whoever is on duty this morning is tired from the weekend and doesn't notice the damage," I say. None of us care to speculate how much we might have to pay if the damaged fender is blamed on us.

"Let's hope you're right," Monica says.

We can see the terminal not too far away and begin to walk in that direction. In less than fifteen minutes we arrive and enter the airport. Although the time is 5:45AM, other passengers are already here, and by 6:00AM the *Volotea* check-in desk is open. During the check-in process, we weigh our luggage and trust that each bag that we are checking meets the weight requirements of twenty kilograms. We definitely do not wish to pay a penalty. I am especially pleased when the scale reads seventeen kilograms for my bag, which has a bottle of vino inside. We also weigh our carry-ons, which are restricted to less than ten kilograms each; all of ours are within the parameters. "Great, all our bags are under the limit," Monica says, "now we don't have to worry about it anymore."

"Okay, now to find our gate," Rick says. Departure boards indicate the gate for our scheduled 7:00AM flight, and we make our way toward it. With a little time to spare, we purchase beverages and wait to board our Volotea flight. After a short while an agent announces that the flight is ready to board. We exit the terminal from where a shuttle bus takes us to a spot farther away on the tarmac. Here we board our aircraft without problems.

By 7:10AM the plane is in the sky as the sun rises over Sicily. What a gorgeous sight and perfect scene to etch into my memory as I leave this Italian island where I feel so at home. I am comforted by the thought that I will return.

About the Author

Margie Miklas is a writer, photographer, and critical-care nurse who has a passion for travel, with a particular love of Italy and all things Italian. She writes for *La Gazzetta Italiana*, a monthly newspaper based in her home town of Cleveland, Ohio.

Margie works part-time in a cardiovascular intensive care unit, and looks ahead to retirement later this year. She is always seeking out opportunities to travel, especially to Italy. She lives in Port St Lucie, Florida, where she enjoys spending time with her twin granddaughters, as well as going to the beach when she is not writing.

Margie writes a blog, margieinitaly, where you can follow her adventures throughout Italy. *My Love Affair with Sicily* is Margie's second book and is based on her personal experiences during five separate trips to this region of Italy.

She is currently writing her first novel, *Critical Cover-Up*, a medical thriller.

Contact Margie at:
margieeee@comcast.net

Follow Margie on:
https://twitter.com/MargieMiklas
https://www.facebook.com/MargieMiklasAuthor
http://www.amazon.com/Margie-Miklas/e/B0094YY3LA
http://www.pinterest.com/margiemiklas/